ECONOMIC SURVEY 2018-19 & BUDGET 2019-20

An Analysis

Includes

Economic Current Affairs &
Government Programmes & Policies

G. K. PUBLICATIONS (P) LTD.

CL MEDIA (P) LTD.

Edition : 2019

Administrative and Production Offices

Published by : **CL Media (P) Ltd.**

A-45, Mohan Cooperative Industrial Area, Near Mohan Estate Metro Station, New Delhi - 110044

ISBN **: 978-93-89310-47-4**

Typeset by : *CL Media DTP Unit*

Marketed by : **G.K. Publications (P) Ltd.**

A-45, Mohan Cooperative Industrial Area, Near Mohan Estate Metro Station, New Delhi - 110044

For product information :

Visit **www.gkpublications.com** or email to **gkp@gkpublications.com**

Word to the Reader

The analysis of Economic Survey and Budget are important for various competitive examinations.

This book provides a overall view of the direction of the Survey and the highlights of the budget. It also contains the address of the President of India regarding the economy and also key government policies, programmes of the Union government.

This book will be a handy tool for aspirants appearing in various examinations in the coming months.

We wish readers all the best in their endeavours.

Contents

5. Science & Technology   5.1-5.13

Economic Survey : 2018-19

The Union Minister for Finance and Corporate Affairs, Smt. Nirmala Sitharaman tabled the Economic Survey 2018-19 in the Parliament today. The Key Highlights of Economic Survey 2018-19 are as follows :

❑ **Shifting gears :** *Private Investment as the Key Driver of Growth, Jobs, Exports and Demand*

- Survey states that pathways for trickle-down opened up during the last five years; and benefits of growth and macroeconomic stability reached the bottom of the pyramid.

- Sustained real GDP growth rate of 8% needed for a $5 trillion economy by 2024-25.

- "Virtuous Cycle" of savings, investment and exports catalyzed and supported by a favorable demographic phase required for sustainable growth.

❑ **Private investment :** *key driver for demand, capacity, labor productivity, new technology, creative destruction and job creation.*

- Survey departs from traditional Anglo-Saxon thinking by viewing the economy as being either in a virtuous or a vicious cycle, and thus never in equilibrium.

- *Key ingredients for a self-sustaining virtuous cycle* :
  - Presenting data as a public good.
- Emphasizing legal reforms.
- Ensuring policy consistency.
- Encouraging behavior change using principles of behavioral economics.
- Nourishing MSMEs to create more jobs and become more productive.
- Reducing the cost of capital.
- Rationalizing the risk-return trade-off for investments.

❑ **Policy for Real People, Not Robots** : *Leveraging the Behavioral Economics of "Nudge"*

- Decisions by real people deviate from impractical robots theorized in classical economics.
- Behavioral economics provides insights to 'nudge' people towards desirable behavior.
- Key principles of behavioral economics:
- Emphasizing the beneficial social norm.
- Changing the default option.
- Repeated reinforcements.

❑ **Using insights from behavioral economics to create an aspirational agenda for social change :**

- From 'Beti Bachao Beti Padhao' to 'BADLAV' (Beti Aapki Dhan Lakshmi Aur Vijay Lakshmi).
- From 'Swachh Bharat' to 'Sundar Bharat'.
- From 'Give it up" for the LPG subsidy to 'Think about the Subsidy'.
- From 'Tax evasion' to 'Tax compliance'.

❑ **Nourishing Dwarfs to become Giants** : *Reorienting policies for MSME Growth*

- Survey focuses on enabling MSMEs to grow for achieving greater profits, job creation and enhanced productivity.

- Dwarfs (firms with less than 100 workers) despite being more than 10 years old, account for more than 50% of all organized firms in manufacturing by number.

- Contribution of dwarfs to employment is only 14% and to productivity is a mere 8%.

- Large firms (more than 100 employees) account for 75% employment and close to 90% of productivity despite accounting for about 15% by number.

- *Unshackling MSMEs and enabling them to grow by way of*:
  - ➢ A sunset clause of less than 10 years, with necessary grand-fathering, for all size-based incentives.
  - ➢ Deregulating labor law restrictions to create significantly more jobs, as evident from Rajasthan.
  - ➢ Re-calibrating Priority Sector Lending (PSL) guidelines for direct credit flow to young firms in high employment elastic sectors.

- Survey also focuses on service sectors such as tourism, with high spillover effects on other sectors such as hotel & catering, transport, real estate, entertainment etc., for job creation.

❑ **Data "Of the People, By the People, For the People"**

- Society's optimal consumption of data is higher than ever given technolo-gical advances in gathering and storage of data.

- As data of societal interest is generated by the people, data can be created as a public good within the legal framework of data privacy.

- Government must intervene in creating data as a public good, especially of the poor and in social sectors.

- Merging the distinct datasets held by the Government already would generate multiple benefits.

❑ **Ending Matsyanyaya** : *How to Ramp up Capacity in the Lower Judiciary*

- Delays in contract enforcement and disposal resolution are arguably now the single biggest hurdle to the ease of doing business and higher GDP growth in India.

- Around 87.5 per cent of pending cases are in the District and Subordinate courts.

- 100 per cent clearance rate can be achieved by filling out merely 2279 vacancies in the lower courts and 93 in High Courts.

- States of Uttar Pradesh, Bihar, Odisha and West Bengal need special attention.

- Productivity improvements of 25 percent in lower courts, 4 percent in High Courts and 18 percent in Supreme Court can clear backlog.

❑ **How does Policy Uncertainty affect Investment ?**

- Significant reduction in Economic Policy Uncertainty in India over the last one decade, even when economic policy uncertainty increased in major countries, especially the U.S.

- Uncertainty dampens investment growth in India for about five quarters.

- Lower economic policy uncertainty can foster a salutary investment climate.

- Survey proposes reduction in economic policy uncertainty by way of:

  ➢ Consistency of actual policy with forward guidance.

  ➢ Quality assurance certification of processes in Government departments.

❑ **India's Demography at 2040** : *Planning Public Good Provision for the 21st Century*

- Sharp slowdown in population growth expected in next 2 decades. Most of India to enjoy demographic dividend while some states will transition to ageing societies by 2030s.

- National Total Fertility Rate expected to be below replacement rate by 2021.

- Working age population to grow by roughly 9.7mn per year during 2021-31 and 4.2mn per year during 2031-41.

- Significant decline to be witnessed in elementary school-going children (5-14 age group) over next two decades.

- States need to consolidate/merge schools to make them viable rather than build new ones.

- Policy makers need to prepare for ageing by investing in health care and by increasing the retirement age in a phased manner.

❑ **From Swachh Bharat to Sundar Bharat via Swasth Bharat :** *An Analysis of the Swachh Bharat Mission*

- Traceable health benefits brought about by Swachh Bharat Mission (SBM).

- 93.1% of the households have access to toilets.

- 96.5% of those with access to toilets are using them in rural India.

- 100% Individual Households Latrine (IHHL) Coverage in 30 states and UTs.

- Financial savings from a household toilet exceed the financial costs to the household by 1.7 times on average and 2.4 times for poorest households.

- Environmental and water management issues need to be incorporated in SBM for sustainable improvements in the long-term.

❑ **Enabling Inclusive Growth through Affordable, Reliable and Sustainable Energy**

- 2.5 times increase in per capita energy consumption needed for India to increase its real per capita GDP by $5000 at 2010 prices, and enter the upper-middle income group.

- 4 times increase in per capita energy consumption needed for India to achieve 0.8 Human Development Index score.

- India now stands at 4th in wind power, 5th in solar power and 5th in renewable power installed capacity.

- Rs 50,000 crore saved and 108.28 million tonnes of CO_2 emissions reduced by energy efficiency programmes in India.

- Share of renewable (excluding hydro above 25 MW) in total electricity generation increased from 6% in 2014-15 to 10% in 2018-19.

- Thermal power still plays a dominant role at 60% share.

- Market share of electric cars only 0.06% in India while it is 2% in China and 39% in Norway.

- Access to fast battery charging facilities needed to increase the market share of electric vehicles.

❑ **Effective Use of Technology for Welfare Schemes – Case of MGNREGS**

- Survey says that efficacy of MGNREGS increased with use of technology in streamlining it.

- Significant reduction in delays in the payment of wages with adoption of NeFMS and DBT in MGNREGS.

- Demand and supply of work under MGNREGS increased, especially in distressed districts.

- Vulnerable sections of the society viz. women, SC and ST workforce increased under MGNREGS during economic distress.

❑ **Redesigning a Minimum Wage System in India for Inclusive Growth**

- Survey proposes a well-designed minimum wage system as a potent tool for protecting workers and alleviating poverty.

- Present minimum wage system in India has 1,915 minimum wages for various scheduled job categories across states.

- 1 in every 3 wage workers in India not protected by the minimum wage law.

- Survey supports rationalization of minimum wages as proposed under the Code on Wages Bill.

- Minimum wages to all employments/workers proposed by the Survey.

- 'National Floor Minimum Wage' should be notified by the Central Government, varying across five geographical regions.

- Minimum wages by states should be fixed at levels not lower than the 'floor wage'.

- Minimum wages can be notified based either on the skills or on geographical region or on both grounds.

- Survey proposes a simple and enforceable Minimum Wage System using technology.

- 'National level dashboard' under the Ministry of Labour & Employment for regular notifications on minimum wages, proposed by the Survey.

- Toll-free number to register grievance on non-payment of the statutory minimum wages.

- Effective minimum wage policy as an inclusive mechanism for more resilient and sustainable economic development.

❑ **State of the Economy in 2018-19 : A Macro View**

- India still the fastest growing major economy in 2018-19.

- Growth of GDP moderated to 6.8 per cent in 2018-19 from 7.2 per cent in 2017-18.

- Inflation contained at 3.4 per cent in 2018-19.

- Non-Performing Assets as percentage of Gross Advances reduced to 10.1 per cent at end December 2018 from 11.5 per cent at end March 2018.

- *Investment growth recovering since* 2017-18 :

  ➢ Growth in fixed investment picked up from 8.3 per cent in 2016-17 to 9.3 per cent next year and further to 10.0 per cent in 2018-19.

- Current account deficit manageable at 2.1 percent of GDP.

- Fiscal deficit of Central Government declined from 3.5 percent of GDP in 2017-18 to 3.4 percent in 2018-19.

- Prospects of pickup in growth in 2019-20 on the back of further increase in private investment and acceleration in consumption.

❏ **Fiscal Developments**

- FY 2018-19 ended with fiscal deficit at 3.4 per cent of GDP and debt to GDP ratio of 44.5 per cent (Provisional).

- As per cent of GDP, total Central Government expenditure fell by 0.3 percentage points in 2018-19 PA over 2017-18 :

  ➢ 0.4 percentage point reduction in revenue expenditure and 0.1 percentage point increase in capital expenditure.

- States' own tax and non-tax revenue displays robust growth in 2017-18 RE and envisaged to be maintained in 2018-19 BE.

- General Government (Centre plus states) on the path of fiscal consolidation and fiscal discipline.

- The revised fiscal glide path envisages achieving fiscal deficit of 3 per cent of GDP by FY 2020-21 and Central Government debt to 40 per cent of GDP by 2024-25.

❏ **Money Management and Financial Intermediation**

- Banking system improved as NPA ratios declined and credit growth accelerated.

- Insolvency and Bankruptcy Code led to recovery and resolution of significant amount of distressed assets and improved business culture.

  ➤ Till March 31, 2019, the CIRP yielded a resolution of 94 cases involving claims worth INR 1,73,359 crore.

  ➤ As on 28 Feb 2019, 6079 cases involving INR 2.84 lakh crores have been withdrawn.

  ➤ As per RBI reports, INR 50,000 crore received by banks from previously non-performing accounts.

  ➤ Additional INR 50,000 crore "upgraded" from non-standard to standard assets.

- Benchmark policy rate first hiked by 50 bps and later reduced by 75 bps last year.

- Liquidity conditions remained systematically tight since September 2018 thus impacting the yields on government papers.

- Financial flows remained constrained because of decline in the equity finance raised from capital markets and stress in the NBFC sector.

  ➤ Capital mobilized through public equity issuance declined by 81 per cent in 2018-19.

  ➤ Credit growth rate y-o-y of the NBFCs declined from 30 per cent in March 2018 to 9 per cent in March 2019.

❏ **Prices and Inflation**

- Headline inflation based on CPI-C continuing on its declining trend for fifth straight financial year remained below 4.0 per cent in the last two years.

- Food inflation based on Consumer Food Price Index (CFPI) also continuing on its declining trend for fifth financial year has remained below 2.0 per cent for the last two consecutive years.

- CPI-C based core inflation (CPI excluding the food and fuel group) has now started declining since March 2019 after increment during FY 2018-19 as compared to FY 2017-18.

- Miscellaneous, housing and fuel and light groups are the main contributors of headline inflation based on CPI-C during FY 2018-19 and the importance of services in shaping up headline inflation has increased.

- CPI rural inflation declined during FY 2018-19 over FY 2017-18. However, CPI urban inflation increased marginally during FY 2018-19. Many States witnessed fall in CPI inflation during FY 2018-19.

❑ **Sustainable Development and Climate Change**

- *India's SDG Index Score ranges between 42 and 69 for States and between 57 and 68 for UTs* :

  ➢ Kerala and Himachal Pradesh are the front runners with a score of 69 amongst states.

  ➢ Chandigarh and Puducherry are the front runners with a score of 68 and 65 respectively among the UTs.

❑ **Namami Gange Mission** launched as a key policy priority towards achieving the SDG 6, with a budget outlay of INR. 20,000 crore for the period 2015-2020.

❑ For mainstreaming Resource Efficiency approach in the development pathway for achieving SDGs, a national policy on Resource Efficiency should be devised.

❑ **A comprehensive NCAP launched in 2019 as a pan India time bound strategy for :**

- Prevention, control and abatement of air pollution

- Augmenting the air quality monitoring network across the country.

❑ **Achievements in CoP 24 in Katowice, Poland in 2018 :**

- Recognition of different starting points for developed and developing countries.

- Flexibilities for developing countries.

- Consideration of principles including equity and Common but Differentiated Responsibilities and Respective Capabilities.

❑ **Paris Agreement also emphasizes the role of climate finance without which the proposed NDCs would not fructify.**

- Though the international community witnessed various claims by developed countries about climate finance flows, the actual amount of flows is far from these claims.

- Scale and size of investments required to implement India's NDC requires mobilizing international public finance and private sector resources along with domestic public budgets.

❑ **External Sector**

- As per WTO, World trade growth slowed down to 3 per cent in 2018 from 4.6 per cent in 2017. Reasons:
  - ➢ Introduction of new and retaliatory tariff measures.
  - ➢ Heightened US-China trade tensions.
  - ➢ Weaker global economic growth.
  - ➢ Volatility in financial markets (WTO).

- In Indian rupee terms growth rate of exports increased owing to depreciation of the rupee while that of imports declined in 2018-19.

- Net capital inflows moderated in April-December of 2018-19 despite robust foreign direct investment (FDI) inflows, outweighed by withdrawals under portfolio investment.

- India's **External Debt** was US$ 521.1 billion at end-December 2018, 1.6 per cent lower than its level at end-March 2018.

- The key external debt indicators reflect that India's external debt is not unsustainable.

- **The total liabilities-to-GDP ratio,** inclusive of both debt and non-debt components, has declined from 43 per cent in 2015 to about 38 per cent at end of 2018.

- The share of foreign direct investment has risen and that of net portfolio investment fallen in total liabilities, reflecting a transition to more stable sources of funding the current account deficit.

- The Indian Rupee traded in the range of 65-68 per US$ in 2017-18 but depreciated to a range of 70-74 in 2018-19.

- The income terms of trade, a metric that measures the purchasing power to import, has been on a rising trend, possibly because the growth of crude prices has still not exceeded the growth of India's export prices.

- The exchange rate in 2018-19 has been more volatile than in the previous year, mainly due to volatility in crude prices, but not much due to net portfolio flows.

- **Composition of India's exports and import basket in 2018-19(P) :**

  - **Exports (including re-exports) :** INR 23,07,663 Cr.

  - **Imports :** INR 35,94,373 Cr.

  - **Top export items** continue to be Petroleum products, precious stones, drug formulations, gold and other precious metals.

  - **Top import items** continue to be Crude petroleum, pearl, precious, semi-precious stones and gold.

  - **India's main trading partners** continue to be the US, China, Hong Kong, the UAE and Saudi Arabia.

- India has signed 28 bilateral / multilateral trade agreements with various country/group of countries. In 2018-19,

  - Exports to these countries stood at US$121.7 billion accounting for 36.9 per cent of India's total exports.

  - Imports from these countries stood at US$266.9 billion accounting for 52.0 per cent of India's total imports.

❑ Agriculture and Food Management

- Agriculture sector in India typically goes through cyclical movement in terms of its growth.

  - ➢ Gross Value Added (GVA) in agriculture improved from a negative 0.2 per cent in 2014-15 to 6.3 per cent in 2016-17 but decelerated to 2.9 per cent in 2018-19.

- Gross Capital Formation (GCF) in agriculture as percentage of GVA marginally declined to 15.2 per cent in 2017-18 as compared to 15.6 per cent in 2016-17.

- The public sector GCF in agriculture as a percentage of GVA increased to 2.7 per cent in 2016-17 from 2.1 per cent in 2013-14.

- Women's participation in agriculture increased to 13.9 per cent in 2015-16 from 11.7 per cent in 2005-06 and their concentration is highest (28 per cent) among small and marginal farmers.

- A shift is seen in the number of operational land holdings and area operated by operational land holdings towards small and marginal farmers.

- 89% of groundwater extracted is used for irrigation. Hence, focus should shift from land productivity to 'irrigation water productivity'. Thrust should be on micro-irrigation to improve water use efficiency.

- Fertilizer response ratio has been declining over time. Organic and natural farming techniques including Zero Budget Natural Farming (ZBNF) can improve both water use efficiency and soil fertility.

- Adopting appropriate technologies through Custom Hiring Centers and implementation of ICT are critical to improve resource-use efficiency among small and marginal farmers.

- Diversification of livelihoods is critical for inclusive and sustainable development in agriculture and allied sectors. Policies should focus on

➢ Dairying as India is the largest producer of milk.

➢ Livestock rearing particularly of small ruminants.

➢ Fisheries sector, as India is the second largest producer.

❑ **Industry and Infrastructure**

- Overall Index of Eight Core Industries registered a growth rate of 4.3 percent in 2018-19.

- India's ranking improved by 23 to 77th position in 2018 among 190 countries assessed by the World Bank Doing Business (DB) Report, 2019.

- Road construction grew @ 30 km per day in 2018-19 compared to 12 km per day in 2014-15.

- Rail freight and passenger traffic grew by 5.33 per cent and 0.64 per cent respectively in 2018-19 as compared to 2017-18.

- Total telephone connections in India touched 118.34 crore in 2018-19

- The installed capacity of electricity has increased to 3,56,100 MW in 2019 from 3, 44,002 MW in 2018.

- Public Private Partnerships are quintessential for addressing infrastructure gaps

- Building sustainable and resilient infrastructure has been given due importance with sector specific flagship programmes such as SAUBHAGYA scheme, PMAY etc

- Institutional mechanism is needed to deal with time-bound resolution of disputes in infrastructure sector

❑ **Services Sector**

- Services sector (excluding construction) has a share of 54.3 per cent in India's GVA and contributed more than half of GVA growth in 2018-19.

- The IT-BPM industry grew by 8.4 per cent in 2017-18 to US$ 167 billion and is estimated to reach US$ 181 billion in 2018-19.

- The services sector growth declined marginally to 7.5 per cent in 2018-19 from 8.1 per cent in 2017-18.
  - ➢ Accelerated sub-sectors: Financial services, real estate and professional services.
  - ➢ Decelerated sub-sectors: Hotels, transport, communication and broadcasting services.
  - ➢ Services share in employment is 34 per cent in 2017.

❑ **Tourism**

- 10.6 million foreign tourists received in 2018-19 compared to 10.4 million in 2017-18.

- Forex earnings from tourism stood at US$ 27.7 billion in 2018-19 compared to US$ 28.7 billion in 2017-18.

❑ **Social Infrastructure, Employment and Human Development**

- The public investments in social infrastructure like education, health, housing and connectivity is critical for inclusive development.

- Government expenditure (Centre plus States) as a percentage of GDP on

- **Health :** increased to 1.5 per cent in 2018-19 from 1.2 per cent in 2014-15.

- **Education :** increased from 2.8 per cent to 3 per cent during this period.

- Substantial progress in both quantitative and qualitative indicators of education is reflected in the improvements in Gross Enrolment Ratios, Gender Parity Indices and learning outcomes at primary school levels.

- **Encouraging Skill Development by** :

  - ➤ Introduction of the skill vouchers as a financing instrument to enable youth obtain training from any accredited training institutes.

  - ➤ Involving industry in setting up of training institutes in PPP mode; in curriculum development; provision of equipment; training of trainers etc.

  - ➤ Personnel of Railways and para-military could be roped in for imparting training in difficult terrains.

  - ➤ Create a database of Instructors, skill mapping of rural youth by involving local bodies to assess the demand-supply gaps are some of the other initiatives proposed.

- Net employment generation in the formal sector was higher at 8.15 lakh in March, 2019 as against 4.87 lakh in February, 2018 as per EPFO.

- Around 1, 90, 000 km of rural roads constructed under Pradhan Mantri Gram Sadak Yojana (PMGSY) since 2014.

- About 1.54 crore houses completed under Pradhan Mantri Awas Yojana (PMAY) as against a target of 1 crore pucca houses with basic amenities by 31st March, 2019.

- Accessible, affordable and quality healthcare being provided through National Health Mission and Ayushman Bharat scheme for a healthy India.

- Alternative healthcare, National AYUSH Mission launched to provide cost effective and equitable AYUSH healthcare throughout the country to address the issue of affordability, by improving access to these services.

- Employment generation scheme, MGNREGA is prioritized by increasing actual expenditure over the budgetary allocation and an upward trend in budget allocation in the last four years.

Address by the President of India, Shri Ram Nath Kovind to the Joint Sitting of Two Houses of Parliament

1. I am pleased to address the first joint sitting of Parliament after the election of the 17th Lok Sabha, in the year commemorating the 150th birth anniversary of Mahatma Gandhi. I extend my heartiest congratulations to all newly elected Members of this Lok Sabha.

2. More than 61 crore voters of the country set a new record by casting their votes and enhanced the credibility of India's democracy in the world. People have stood in long queues braving extreme heat to cast their votes. This time, as compared to previous elections, more women have cast their votes and their participation has been almost equal to men. Crores of youth have voted for the first time and played an important role in shaping India's future. All voters deserve to be congratulated for the success of this election.

3. I also convey my best wishes to the new Speaker of the Lok Sabha for this new responsibility.

4. I congratulate the entire team of the Election Commission for successful completion of the world's largest election. The contribution of employees of several administrative departments and various institutions, as well as the security

forces in successful conduct of the electoral process is extremely praiseworthy.

5.   Nearly half of the MPs in this Lok Sabha have been elected for the first time. The election of 78 women MPs which is the highest number in the history of Lok Sabha, presents the picture of a New India.

6.   It is a matter of joy that the reflection of India's diversity is visible in this joint sitting. People of every age, hailing from villages and cities, belonging to every profession, are members of both the Houses. Many members are associated with social service, many are from the field of agriculture, from business and economic sphere while other members are from the field of education, medical profession which saves the lives of people and legal profession which provides justice to the people. MPs who have made their mark in the world of cinema, art, literature and culture are also present here. I am confident that your unique experiences will contribute to enriching the discussions in Parliament.

7.   The people of the country have given a very clear mandate in this election. After assessing the performance of the Government during the first tenure, the people have given even stronger support for the second term. By doing so, the people of the country have given a mandate for continuing uninterrupted and at an accelerated pace the journey of development which started in 2014.

8.   All fellow countrymen are familiar with the atmosphere prevailing in the country before 2014. In order to take the country out of a sense of gloom and instability, the people elected a Government with absolute majority after three decades. Giving the highest regard to that mandate, my Government started to march forward without any discrimination with the mantra of 'Sabka Saath- Sabka Vikas', to create a New India.

9.   On January 31st this year, in this very Central Hall, I had said that my Government from the very first day was dedicated to the goal of improving the lives of all citizens, addressing their problems arising out of mis-governance and providing all basic amenities to the last person standing at the margins of society.

10. During the last five years, the countrymen have come to believe that the Government is always with them, working to improve their lives and to enhance their Ease of Living. Based on this wealth of people's trust, a fresh mandate was sought.

11. People of the country have long waited for the basic amenities of life. But now the conditions are changing. My Government wants to make the people conscious, capable, well-provided and unfettered to such an extent that that they do not feel the "Burden, Force, or Absence" of the Government in their daily life. Empowering every person in the country is the main goal of my Government.

12. My Government is committed to that very idea of nation-building, the foundation for which was laid in 2014. While fulfilling the basic needs of the countrymen, now the Government is moving forward towards realising their aspirations of building a Strong, Safe, Prosperous and All-inclusive India. This journey is inspired by the basic spirit of 'Sabka Saath, Sabka Vikas aur Sabka Vishwas'.

    This New India's vision is motivated by the noble thoughts ofShri Narayana Guru Kerala's great spiritual figure, social reformer and poet:

    "Jaati-Bhedam Mat-Dwesham AdumIlladey Sarvrum

    Sodar-tvain Vaadunn Matrukasthan Maanit"

    That is, an ideal place is one where people live like brothers free from the discrimination of caste and religion.

13. Three weeks ago, on 30th May, immediately after swearing-in the Government has started working towards building a New India. A New India:

    ● Where equal opportunities to progress are available to every person;

    ● Where life of every person becomes better and their self-esteem is enhanced;

    ● Where brotherhood and harmony bind the people with each other;

- Where the foundation built on our ideals and values becomes stronger; and

- Where the benefits of development reach every region and the last person standing in the queue.

This New India, will move forward towards that ideal state envisioned by Gurudev Rabindra Nath Tagore, where the mind of the people is without fear and the head is held high with self-esteem. In Gurudev's words:

"Chitto Jetha Bhay-Shunno, Uchcho Jetha Shir."

14. It is a matter of pride for every Indian that when our country completes 75 years of independence in 2022, we would have achieved many national goals for building a New India. To pave the way for the golden future of New India, my Government has resolved:

On this path of a New India, the rural India will be strong and urban India will also be empowered;

- On this path of a New India, the entrepreneurial India will attain new heights and the dreams of young India will also be fulfilled;

- On this path of a New India, all systems will be transparent and the prestige of honest countrymen will increase further;

- On this path of a New India, infrastructure for the 21st century will be built and all resources for creation of a powerful India will be mobilised.

In the light of these resolutions, in a short period of 21 days, my Government has taken many decisions aimed at the welfare of farmers, soldiers, students, entrepreneurs, women and other sections of society and have also started implementing them. Initiatives have also been taken to enact several new laws.

15. A decision has been taken to increase the income support to farmers who are our Annadaata, by extending the coverage under 'Pradhan Mantri Kisan Samman Nidhi', to every farmer in the country. To enable the farmer brothers and sisters who work day and night in their fields to lead a respectable life after attaining the age of 60 years, a 'Pension Scheme' for them has also been approved.

16. Livestock is invaluable for farmers. They have to spend a lot of money for treatment of cattle-related diseases. To reduce this expenditure, my Government has also decided to start a special scheme with an allocation of Rs 13,000 crore.

17. For the first time, a Government has taken note of the economic security of small shopkeepers. In the very first meeting of the Cabinet, a separate 'Pension Scheme' has been approved for small shopkeepers and retail traders. About 3 crore small shopkeepers in the country will benefit from this scheme.

18. We are all indebted to the soldiers who dedicate themselves to protect the countrymen by sacrificing every joy, every pleasure and every festive occasion. It is our duty to secure the future of children of those who guard the border, and ensure peace and security for everyone. Inspired by this sentiment, the amount of scholarship under the 'National Defence Fund' has been increased for the children of our brave soldiers. For the first time, sons and daughters of the State police personnel have also been included in this scholarship.

19. One of the biggest challenges of the 21st century is – the growing water crisis. Over time, the traditional and effective practices of water conservation in our country are disappearing. Houses have come up over ponds and lakes, and the vanishing water sources have accentuated the water crisis for the poor. In view of the growing impact of Climate Change and Global Warming, water crisis is likely to aggravate further. Today, the need of the hour is that the way the country has shown seriousness about 'Swachh Bharat Abhiyaan', the same seriousness be shown in 'Water Conservation and Management'.

20. We must conserve water for our children and future generations. The creation of the new 'Ministry of Jalshakti' is a decisive step in this direction, which will have far-reaching benefits. Through this new Ministry, the systems related to water conservation and management will be made more effective.

21. My Government is fully conscious of the crisis in the drought-hit areas and stands by every affected citizen. With the support of State Governments and Sarpanches at the village level, it is being ensured that farmers are assisted and the scarcity of drinking water is tackled.

22. Strengthening the system and spirit of Co-operative Federalism, my Government is taking the States along to achieve the national goals. Last week, important developmental issues were discussed with the Chief Ministers and a decision was taken to constitute a Committee of Chief Ministers to look into Structural Reforms in the field of agriculture.

23. Only on the foundation of a strong rural economy, it is possible to build a strong national economy. Our farmers are the pillars of rural economy. All possible efforts are being made by the Central Government to provide adequate assistance to the States for agricultural development.

24. Large scale investments have been made to strengthen rural India. In order to enhance agriculture productivity, an investment of Rs. 25 lakh crore will be made in the coming years.

25. To double the income of farmers by 2022, several steps have been taken in the last 5 years. Be it the decision to increase the MSP, or approval for 100 percent FDI in food processing; be it completion of the irrigation projects pending for decades or extension of 'Crop Insurance Scheme'; be it the 'Soil Health Card' or 100% Neem coating of urea; my Government has taken many decisions, appreciating such numerous small and big needs of the farmers. The Government has made the agriculture policy both production-centric as well as income-centric.

26. An important link in these efforts is 'Pradhan Mantri Kisan Samman Nidhi'. Through this, an amount of more than Rs. 12,000 crore has been disbursed to the farmers in just three months. An estimated expenditure of Rs. 90,000 crore is likely to be incurred annually on this scheme since every farmer has now been brought in its ambit.

27. With the provision of storage for farm produce, the economic security of the farmers is strengthened. Now the storage facility will be provided to the farmers near their village through the 'Grameen Bhandaran Yojana'.

28. The benefit of cooperatives in the agriculture sector is being availed by the farmers in the dairy business. In other areas of agriculture also, the target is to create 10,000 new 'Farmer Producer Organisations' to benefit the farmers.

29. Today, India is second in the world in fish production. Our country has the potential to attain the first place. There is immense potential for increasing the income of farmers through marine fish industry and inland fisheries. That is why the Government is committed to 'Neeli Kranti' which means 'Blue Revolution'. A separate Department has been constituted for integrated development of fisheries. Similarly, a special fund has been created to develop infrastructure related to fishing industry.

30. We can achieve our constitutional objectives only by liberating the poor families of the country from poverty. During the last five years, the schemes implemented in the country for the welfare of farmers, labourers, divyangjan, tribals and women have achieved wide spread success. Only by empowering the poor can they be rescued from the vicious cycle of poverty. That is why the Government has adopted an approach to empower the poor, deprived and weaker sections through provision of housing, healthcare, essential amenities of life, financial inclusion, education, skill and self-employment. This is in harmony with Deen Dayal Upadhyaya's concept of Antyodaya.

31. Comprehensive work is underway for the development of 112 'Aspirational Districts' in the country. 1 lakh 15 thousand most backward villages of the country are in these districts. With the development of education and healthcare facilities and infrastructure in these villages, there will be a positive impact on the lives of crores of poor families.

32. After the success of the world's largest financial inclusion campaign, in the form of 'Jan-Dhan Yojana', my Government is also working to bring the banking services to the doorsteps of the people. In order to ensure that banking services are

readily available in every village of the country and in the inaccessible areas of North East, work is being done at a fast pace. About 1.5 lakh post offices in the country are being prepared to provide banking services through 'India Post Payment Bank'. Our goal is to utilise the postman as a mobile bank to bring banking services to every doorstep.

33. Cost of medical treatment pushes the poor families into financial crisis. In order to protect them from this crisis, world's biggest healthcare scheme 'Ayushman Bharat Yojana' has been implemented, providing 'Health-Protection-Cover' to 50 crore poor people. Under this, so far about 26 lakh poor patients have availed treatment in hospitals. In order to provide medicines at affordable rates, 5,300 'Jan Aushadhi Kendras' have also been opened. It is our endeavour to provide medicines at affordable rates to people residing in far-flung areas through these Jan Aushadhi Kendras.

34. The objective is to set up about 1.5 lakh 'Health and Wellness Centres' in all rural areas by 2022. So far, about 18,000 such Centres have already been operationalised.

35. Our countrymen can learn a lot from tribal communities. Our tribal brothers and sisters live in harmony with the environment and nature and maintain a beautiful balance between development and tradition. In New India, every effort will be made to create an inclusive and sensitive system in the interest of tribal communities. Many schemes have been implemented for all-round development of tribal areas. Work is in progress to provide 'Learning to Earning' facilities to the youth residing in the forest areas. In tribal dominated areas, 'Eklavya Model Residential Schools' are being set up for children. The thrust is on value addition and marketing of forest produce through Van Dhan Kendras.

36. Women Empowerment is one of the top priorities of my Government. Empowerment of women and their effective involvement in society and economy is the touchstone of a developed society. The Government's thinking promotes not only women's development but also women-led development. According the highest priority to women's security, several

effective steps have been initiated with the cooperation of the States. Penalties for crimes against women have been made harsher and the new penal provisions are being strictly enforced. The 'Beti Bachao Beti Padhao'campaign has brought down female foeticide and improved the sex ratio in many districts of the country.

37. Rural women are the biggest beneficiaries of freedom from smoke through 'Ujjwala Yojana', vaccination through 'Mission Indradhanush' and free electricity connections under 'Saubhagya' Yojana. Women are also being given priority in the registration of houses built under 'Pradhan Mantri Awas Yojana'in the rural areas. Under this scheme, nearly 2 crore new houses will be built in the villages during the next three years.

38. Facilities for the women workers in the unorganized sector are also being augmented. Self-employment opportunities are being made available to rural women through 'Deen Dayal Upadhyaya Rashtriya Aajivika Mission. Under the 'Rashtriya Aajivika Mission', loans amounting to more than Rs 2 lakh crore have been disbursed so far to 3 crore women in rural areas.

39. My Government is committed to make women equal stakeholders in the country's development and prosperity. Efforts will be made in collaboration with industry and corporate sector to provide better employment opportunities to women. In addition, in Government procurement, priority will be given to those enterprises where women's participation in the workforce is more than the prescribed limit.

40. To secure equal rights for every sister and daughter in the country, eradication of social evils like 'Triple Talaq' and 'Nikah-Halala' is imperative. I would urge all the members to cooperate in these efforts to make the lives of our sisters and daughters better and dignified.

41. Our young generation must have a meaningful participation in the building of New India. In the last five years, attempts have been made for developing the skills of the youth, providing them financial support for start-ups and self-employment, and

making available adequate number of seats for higher education. The amount of scholarship has also been increased by 25 per cent.

42. The Government has made provision of 10 per cent reservation for youth from economically weaker section of the general category. This will enable them to get more opportunities in employment and education.

43. To enable the youth of all strata of society to fulfil their dreams, timely provision of financial resources is being emphasised. The impact of 'Pradhan Mantri Mudra Yojna' has been felt on a big scale. Under this scheme, about 19 crore loans have been disbursed for self-employment. An effort will now be made to cover 30 crore people by expanding this scheme. A facility for entrepreneurs to avail loan up to Rs. 50 lakh without any guarantee will also be introduced. Apart from this, new employment opportunities will be generated through appropriate policies in sectors which have the potential to accelerate the economy.

44. Today India has joined the league of countries with most number of start-ups in the world. To improve the start-up ecosystem, the Government is simplifying the rules. This campaign will be further expedited. Our goal is to establish 50,000 start-ups in the country by 2024.

45. Research is being encouraged in higher educational institutions. To further strengthen this effort, it is proposed to establish a 'National Research Foundation'. This proposed foundation will work as a bridge between different Departments of the Central Government, science laboratories, higher educational institutions and industrial institutions.

46. To enable various higher educational institutions of India to find a place in the top 500 educational institutions of the world, they are being encouraged through grant of autonomy and financial assistance.

47. My Government is striving to increase the number of seats in the country's Higher Education System by one-and-a-half times by 2024. With this initiative, 2 crore additional seats would be available for the youth in higher educational institutions.

48. It is our responsibility to provide appropriate opportunities, environment and quality education to enhance the talent of children. In this regard, the 'Pradhan Mantri Innovative Learning Programme' will be started.

49. In order to attract children early enough, at the school level, towards technology, suitable infrastructure is being created. Through the 'Atal Innovation Mission', the work of establishing 'Atal Tinkering Labs' in about 9,000 schools across the country, is progressing rapidly. Similarly, 'Atal Incubation Centres' are being set up in 102 universities and other institutions.

50. Impressive performance in sports competitions at the world level, enhances the pride of the country as well as increases the interest of children and youth in sports. It also strengthens the culture of according primacy to health in life. To make India a global sports powerhouse, it is important that talented players living in far-flung areas of the country are identified and their selection process is made transparent. To identify the players at the state and district level, it has been decided to widen the 'Khelo-India Programme'. Under this, 2,500 talented players have been selected, and are being trained. Now this facility will be provided to 2,500 new players every year.

51. The sports infrastructure in the country will be modernised as well as expanded. A new system is being evolved to make available modern infrastructure and facilities to the players. It is our endeavour that our players win high accolades in the sports world and enhance the prestige of our country.

52. Economic development plays the most vital role in improving the lives of our countrymen. Today India is among the fastest growing economies in the world. Inflation is low, fiscal deficit is under control, foreign exchange reserves are growing and the impact of Make In India is clearly visible.

53. India is now on the way to become the world's 5th largest economy in terms of GDP. To maintain the high growth rate, reform process will continue. It is our objective to make India a 5-trillion dollar economy by 2024.

54. Work is underway in full earnest to transform India into a Global Manufacturing Hub. Keeping in view Industry 4.0, a New Industrial Policy will be announced shortly.In 'Ease of Doing Business', India has leap-frogged 65 positions during the past 5 years, from a ranking of 142 in 2014 to 77. Now our goal is to be among the top 50 countries of the world.In order to achieve this, process of simplification of rules will be further expedited in collaboration with the States. In this sequence, necessary amendments are also being brought in the Companies Law.

55. Taxation regime plays an important role in accelerating economic development. Along with continuous reform, simplification of taxation system is also being emphasised. Exemption to persons earning up to Rs. 5 lakh from payment of income tax is an important step in this direction.

56. Similarly, indirect tax system is also being made simple and effective. With the implementation of GST, the concept of 'One country, One tax, One market' has become a reality. Efforts to further simplify the GST will continue.

57. Keeping in view the interests of small traders, my Government has launched a New Pension Scheme for them. 'National Traders Welfare Board' will be constituted shortly, and 'National Retail Trade Policy' will be formulated to promote retail business. Accident insurance of up to Rs. 10 lakh will also be provided to all traders registered under GST.

58. MSME sector provides a strong foundation to the country's economy, and plays a critical role in employment generation. Several steps have been taken to ensure smooth cash flow to enterprises run by small entrepreneurs. In order to ensure that entrepreneurs associated with MSME sector do not face any problem in accessing credit, the credit guarantee coverage is being enhanced to Rs. 1 lakh crore.

59. Good governance reduces corruption, enhances self-respect of the citizens and enables them to optimally utilize their talents and capabilities.

60. My Government will make the Zero Tolerance Policy against corruption more comprehensive and effective. The mission to eliminate corruption from public life and Government services

will be implemented with greater zeal. Towards this objective, Minimum Government - Maximum Governance will be further emphasised. In addition, use of technology will be maximised to reduce Human Interface. Appointment of Lokpal will also promote transparency.

61. The campaign against black money will be taken forward at a faster pace. During the last two years, 4 lakh 25 thousand Company Directors have been disqualified and the registration of 3 lakh 50 thousand suspicious companies has been revoked.

62. The 'Fugitive and Economic Offenders Act' has proved effective in controlling fugitive economic offenders. Now we are receiving information in this regard from 146 countries, including Switzerland. Of these, we have concluded agreements with 80 countries for automatic exchange of information. We are now receiving information about all those who have stashed black money abroad.

63. The impact of 'Real Estate Regulation Act' or RERA is clearly visible in curbing black money transactions in real estate sector and protecting the interests of the customers; providing huge relief to the middle class families.

64. 'Insolvency and Bankruptcy Code' is among the biggest and most impactful economic reforms undertaken in the country. With the coming into force of this Code, banks and other financial institutions have been able to settle directly or indirectly an amount of more than Rs. 3 lakh 50 thousand crore. This Code has also curbed the tendency of wilfully defaulting on loans taken from banks and other financial institutions.

65. Under the 'Direct Benefit Transfer', funds from more than 400 schemes are being directly credited into the accounts of beneficiaries. During the last five years, Rs. 7 lakh 30 thousand crore have been transferred through DBT. So far, not only has DBT prevented Rs. 1 lakh 41 thousand crore from falling into wrong hands, but it has also enabled deletion of names of about 8 crore ineligible beneficiaries. DBT will be further expanded in the coming days. I would urge the State Governments to use DBT in more and more schemes.

66. Infrastructure will play an important role in ushering in a prosperous India. My Government's continuous endeavour has been to build infrastructure in an eco-friendly manner. Along with concrete, greenery has been made an integral part of the highway and expressway projects. For supply of electricity, optimal utilisation of solar energy is being stressed. Household and industrial wastes are also being used in road construction.

67. In the 21st century economy, the pace and spread of urbanization will continue to increase.Development of urban infrastructure in cities and suburbs will pave the way for economic progress and enhance employment opportunities. My Government is tirelessly working for a modern India, by providing world-class infrastructure and public amenities in villages as well as cities. Special emphasis is being accorded to improving connectivity in the North-East, hilly and tribal areas. In addition to increasing the ease of living of citizens in the North-East; tourism, agriculture and other allied sectors will also benefit from better connectivity. Effective steps are being taken to expand organic farming in the North-East.

68. Under the 'Bharatmala Project', construction or upgradation of about 35,000 kilometers of National Highways is to be undertaken by 2022. In addition, under the 'Sagarmala Project', a network of good quality roads is being constructed in coastal areas and areas adjoining ports.

69. Along with the highways, Government is also working extensively in the area of Railways, Airways and Inland Water ways. Under the'UDAN Scheme', air connectivity to smaller towns is being expanded rapidly.

70. Urban transport infrastructure is being created to cater to present and future requirements. While developing infrastructure, attention is also being given to addressing the challenges posed by pollution. My Government is developing a transport system, which is not only fast and safe, but is also environment friendly. For this, special emphasis is given to Public transport. Metro rail network is being expanded rapidly in several cities. The facility of 'One Nation, One Card' has

been launched to realize the dream of seamless mobility. Similarly, electric vehicles are being promoted to reduce vehicular pollution. The network of electric charging stations is also being expanded rapidly.

71. Modern amenities like gas-grid and I-Ways are being developed at a rapid pace. PNG based domestic fuel and CNG based transportation systems are being developed. In modern India, we are according a special emphasis on production of bio-fuel. Prior to 2014, about 67 crore litres of ethanol was being blended. This year, we have set a target of about 270 crore litres for ethanol blending. Enhancing the use of blended ethanol will not only benefit our farmers but also safeguard the environment. Further, it will reduce import of petroleum products thus saving foreign exchange.

72. My Government is fully devoted to make the flow of Ganga uninterrupted and pollution free. Recently, encouraging evidence of revival of aquatic life at several locations along Ganga have been reported. This year, during the Ardhakumbh in Prayagraj, the cleanliness of Ganga and amenities provided to the devotees have made news throughout the world. My Government has enhanced the dignity and self-esteem of every person who contributed towards the successful organization of Ardhakumbh by honouring them.

73. Under the 'Namami Gange'scheme, my Government will further accelerate the campaign for closure of drains releasing effluents in the river Ganga. On the lines of river Ganga, the Government will also endeavour to clean up other rivers such as Kaveri, Periyar, Narmada, Yamuna, Mahanadi and Godavari.

74. My Government is making earnest efforts for conservation of forests, wildlife and the environment. In recent years, forest and tree cover has increased by more than 1 per cent. During the last five years, protected areas in the country have also increased. In 2014, the number of protected areas in the country was 692, which has now gone up to 868. To address the challenges posed by air pollution,'National Clean Air Programme' has been started in 102 cities.

75. Solar energy plays an important role in reducing the adverse effects of Climate Change and Global Warming. Proactive efforts of India have resulted in the formation of the International Solar Alliance. Through this organization, India is contributing significantly to the development of solar energy in the developing countries of the world.

76. Space Technology plays a central role in improving the lives of the common man, providing early-warning of impending disasters, identifying location of natural resources, providing signals to various means of communication and ensuring national security. It is the endeavour of my Government to maximize the use of space technology for human welfare. Several facilities such as roads, houses for poor, farming or equipment for fishermen have all been linked to space technology.

77. Space technology has helped us in further strengthening our security at land, air and water. Our expertise in accurate weather forecast has improved. This was evidenced during the recent'Cyclone Phani' that struck the eastern coast of the country. Due to accurate information and timely preparation, large scale destruction to life and property was averted.

78. India is marching forward to assume a leadership role in unravelling and comprehending the mysteries of space. Our scientists are involved in the preparations for the launch of'Chandrayaan-2', which will be India's first spacecraft to reach the Moon. We are also making rapid progress towards achieving the goal of sending the first Indian in India's own'Gaganyaan' by 2022.

79. During the Lok Sabha elections, the country attained another milestone, which however, did not receive as much attention as it should have. With the successful testing of'Mission Shakti' a new dimension has been added to India's capability in space technology and security-preparedness. For this, today I once again congratulate our scientists and engineers.

80. The role of technology in the field of security is expanding continuously. Keeping this in view, work is in progress to establish three joint service agencies for space, cyber and special forces. These collaborative efforts will strengthen the security of the country.

81. New India is rapidly moving towards occupying its rightful place in the world community. Today, India has acquired a new image and our relations with other countries have become stronger. It is a matter of immense pleasure that in 2022, India will host the G-20 Summit.

82. The world community enthusiastically supported India's proposal to declare June 21st as 'International Day of Yoga' by the United Nations. At present, several programmes associated with International Day of Yoga are being organized with great enthusiasm in various countries, of which the most important events will be held tomorrow, the 21st June.

83. The world community supports India's position on various issues such as climate change, economic and cyber-crime, action against corruption and black money and energy security. Today the whole world stands with India on the issue of terrorism. Designation of Masood Azhar, responsible for dastardly terrorist attacks on our soil, as a global terrorist by United Nations, is a major testimony to this fact.

84. My Government's "Neighborhood First" policy is an evidence of our approach of according priority to South Asia and countries in the adjoining region. India will play a crucial role in the progress of this region. Accordingly, trade, connectivity and people-to-people contact are being encouraged in this region. The presence of Heads of States and Heads of Governments of 'BIMSTEC' countries, Kyrgyzstan – the current chair of 'Shanghai Cooperation Organisation' and Mauritius during the swearing-in of the new Government is a reflection of this policy.

85. My Government is also conscious of protecting the interests of Indians living and working abroad. Today an Indian, if caught in any crisis abroad, is confident of receiving timely help and relief. Several services ranging from passports to visas have been made easy and accessible.

86. Due to the efforts of my Government, India's philosophy, culture and achievements have got a distinct recognition at the global stage. This year, the 150thbirth anniversary of Mahatma Gandhi, which is being celebrated world over, will provide a

fillip to India's 'Thought Leadership'. Similarly, programmes related to the 550th birth anniversary of Guru Nanak Dev ji, will help spread the light of India's spiritual wisdom throughout the world.

87. New India will be sensitive and also, economically prosperous. But for this to happen, nation's security is of utmost importance. My Government accords top most priority to national security. Therefore, effective steps are being taken to tackle Terrorism and Naxalism.

88. India has amply demonstrated both her intent and capabilities, first through surgical strikes and then through air strikes after the Pulwama attack at terrorist hideouts across the border. In future too, all possible steps will be taken to ensure our security.

89. Illegal infiltrators pose a major threat to our internal security. This is leading to social imbalance in many parts of the country, as well as putting a huge pressure on limited livelihood opportunities. My Government has decided to implement the process of 'National Register of Citizens' on priority basis in areas affected by infiltration. Security along the border will be further strengthened to prevent infiltration.

90. While on the one hand, Government is working to identify the infiltrators, on the other, it is also fully committed to protecting the victims of persecution due to their faith. In this regard, efforts will be made to amend the Citizenship Act while protecting the linguistic, cultural and social identities.

91. My Government is making efforts with complete dedication to provide a safe and peaceful environment to the residents of Jammu and Kashmir. The recently concluded peaceful elections to local bodies and to Lok Sabha have bolstered our efforts. My Government is committed to take all necessary steps for the development of Jammu and Kashmir.

92. My Government is resolutely working to eradicate the menace of Naxalism from the country. Considerable success has been achieved in this direction during the last 5 years. The area affected by Naxalism is reducing continuously. In the coming years, development projects will be expedited in these areas, which will benefit our tribal brothers and sisters residing there.

93. My Government is rapidly taking forward the work of modernisation of the army and the armed forces. India is going to receive the delivery of first 'Rafale' fighter aircraft and 'Apache' helicopters in the near future.

94. Special emphasis is being accorded by the Government to manufacture of modern armaments under 'Make in India'. The policy of indigenously manufacturing weapons such as modern rifles and cannons, tanks and combat aircrafts is being carried forward successfully. 'Defence Corridors' coming up in Uttar Pradesh and Tamil Nadu will further strengthen this mission. While fulfilling our security requirements, export of defence equipment is also being encouraged.

95. Respect towards soldiers and martyrs enhances self-respect and enthusiasm among the forces, and also strengthens our military capabilities. Hence, all possible efforts are being made to take care of our soldiers and their families. Through 'One Rank One Pension', increased pensionary benefits to ex-service men and expansion of health facilities, efforts are being made to improve their living standards.

96. The National War Memorialnear India Gate in Delhi, built by my Government, seven decades after India's independence, is a tribute to the martyrs by a grateful nation. Similarly my Government has set up the 'National Police Memorial' in memory of police personnel who were martyred while safeguarding the security of the country.

97. Inspiration from history guides us towards the future path of nation building. It is our duty to preserve the memory of our nation-builders and gratefully remember them. There have been many such efforts during the last five years. 'Dandi Museum' has been built to honour Pujya Bapu and the historic Dandi March. "Statue of Unity", the tallest statue in the world, has been built as a mark of our gratitude to the Iron Man, Sardar Patel. 'Kranti Mandir' has been set up at the Red Fort in Delhi, as a tribute to Netaji Subhash Chandra Bose and other freedom fighters of Azad Hind Fauj.26 Alipur Road in Delhi, the site of Babasaheb Dr. Bhimrao Ambedkar's Mahaparinirvana has been developed as aNational Memorial. A museum is also being built in Delhi as a mark of respect to the contributions of all former Prime Ministers of the country.

98. My Government, inspired by Sardar Patel, is committed to further strengthen the spirit of 'Ek Bharat, Shreshtha Bharat'. For this, it is essential to accord importance to National Ambitions and Regional Aspirations. All forms of dialogue and cooperation will be encouraged to achieve this. Guided by the principle of 'Sabka Sath, Sabka Vikas aur Sabka Vishwas', it is the endeavour of my Government to ensure that no citizen is left behind in India's journey of development.

99. India had to pass through a long period of subjugation. But throughout this period, Indians kept fighting for independence in different parts of the country. The longing for freedom and willingness to make sacrifices to achieve freedom had never waned. This desire for independence culminated into the 'Quit India Movement' in 1942, when the entire nation was determined to achieve independence and even to sacrifice their lives in this cause. Contributing to the freedom struggle was the only thought behind all the actions of our countrymen. We achieved our independence in 1947 on the strength of this collective spirit.

100. Today, all of us are again at a juncture of creating history. We are striving to launch a new movement for ushering in a new era. Our resolve today will determine the shape of the India of 2047 when we celebrate the centenary of our independence.

101. Today, our country is enriched with the experiences of a 72-year journey since independence. The nation is moving ahead only by learning from these experiences. All of us have to move ahead with the resolve to realise the idea of New India by the year 2022 when we celebrate the 75th anniversary of India's independence. Thus, in the New India in the 75th year of its independence:

- Farmers' income will be doubled;
- Every poor will have a pucca roof over his head;
- Every poor will have access to clean fuel;
- Every poor will have electricity connection;
- No poor will be compelled to defecate in the open;
- Every poor will have access to medical facilities;

- Every village in the country will be connected by roads;

- River Ganga will flow uninterrupted, and pollution free;

- In collaboration with States, India will be close to becoming a $ 5 trillion economy;

- We will be progressing towards joining world's three largest economies;

- An Indian will unfurl the tri-colour in space, entirely on the strength of indigenous resources; and

- We will provide leadership to global development with a new zeal and confidence.

102. If the gap between the public and the Government is reduced, and public partnership is ensured, our countrymen can transform Government schemes and programmes into mass movements. This is the way forward to achieve transformative national goals. Adopting this approach, programmes like the 'Beti-Bachao, Beti-Padhao', and 'Swachh Bharat Abhiyan'evolved into mass movements. On the strength of people's participation, we will also achieve the objective of a New India.

103. It is the belief of my Government that political parties, States and 130 crore countrymen are all committed to India's integrated and accelerated development. Our vibrant democracy has also matured adequately.During the last few decades, due to frequent elections being held in some part of the country or the other, the pace and continuity of development programmes have been impacted. Our countrymen have demonstrated their wisdom by delivering a clear verdict both at State and National issues.'One Nation – Simultaneous Elections' is the need of the hour, which would facilitate accelerated development, thereby benefitting our countrymen. With such a system in place, all political parties, according to their respective ideologies, will be able to better utilise their energy towards development and public welfare. Therefore, I urge all Members of Parliament to seriously ponder over this development oriented proposal of'One Nation - Simultaneous Elections'.

104. This year also marks 70 years of adoption of the Indian Constitution. As a Member of Parliament, all of you have undertaken the oath or affirmation to discharge your duties with true faith and allegiance to the Constitution of India. The Constitution is paramount to all of us. The chief architect of our Constitution, Babasaheb Dr. Bhimrao Ambedkar had said that 'we must hold fast to constitutional methods of achieving our social and economic objectives'.

105. Our Constitution provides guidance for ensuring social, economic and political justice as well as securing liberty and equality for all citizens; and promote fraternity among all, assuring the dignity of the individual.

106. I believe that you all Members of the Rajya Sabha and the Lok Sabha, as parliamentarians, will make invaluable contributions in achieving the ideals of the Constitution while discharging your duties. In this way, you will contribute effectively in ushering in a New India.

107. All of us will have to accord priority to our duties as public representatives and as citizens of the country. Only then will we be able to inspire countrymen to discharge their duties as citizens.

108. My advice to all MPs is that you should always remember the fundamental mantra of Gandhiji. He had said that every decision of ours should be guided by its impact on the poorest and the weakest person in the society. You must also remember the voter who setting aside all his work and overcoming his difficulties went to the polling station to cast his vote and discharge his responsibilities towards the nation. Your priority should be to fulfil his aspirations.

109. I urge you all to dedicate yourselves in the task of building a New India and to discharge your duties with utmost sincerity over the next five years. I once again wish the very best to all of you.

Union Budget : 2019-20

❑ **Key Highlights of Union Budget 2019-20:** *The Union Minister for Finance and Corporate Affairs Smt. Nirmala Sitharaman made her maiden Budget Speech today and presented the Union Budget 2019-20 before the Parliament. The key highlights of Union Budget 2019 are as follows :*

❑ **10-point Vision for the decade**

- Building Team India with Jan Bhagidari: Minimum Government Maximum Governance.

- Achieving green Mother Earth and Blue Skies through a pollution-free India.

- Making Digital India reach every sector of the economy.

- Launching Gaganyan, Chandrayaan, other Space and Satellite programmes.

- Building physical and social infrastructure.

- Water, water management, clean rivers.

- Blue Economy.

- Self-sufficiency and export of food-grains, pulses, oilseeds, fruits and vegetables.

- Achieving a healthy society via Ayushman Bharat, well-nourished women & children, safety of citizens.
- Emphasis on MSMEs, Start-ups, defence manufacturing, automobiles, electronics, fabs and batteries, and medical devices under Make in India.

❑ **Towards a 5 Trillion Dollar Economy**

- "People's hearts filled with Aasha (Hope), Vishwas (Trust), Aakansha (Aspirations)", says FM.
- Indian economy to become a 3 trillion dollar economy in the current year.
- Government aspires to make India a 5 trillion dollar economy.
- "India Inc. are India's job-creators and nation's wealth-creators", says FM.
- **Need for investment in :**
  - ➢ Infrastructure.
  - ➢ Digital economy.
  - ➢ Job creation in small and medium firms.
- Initiatives to be proposed for kick-starting the virtuous cycle of investments.
- Common man's life changed through MUDRA loans for ease of doing business.

❑ **Measures related to MSMEs :**

- **Pradhan Mantri Karam Yogi Maandhan Scheme**
  - ➢ Pension benefits to about three crore retail traders & small shopkeepers with annual turnover less than Rs. 1.5 crore.
  - ➢ Enrolment to be kept simple, requiring only Aadhaar, bank account and a self-declaration.
- Rs. 350 crore allocated for FY 2019-20 for 2% interest subvention (on fresh or incremental loans) to all GST-registered MSMEs, under the Interest Subvention Scheme for MSMEs.

- Payment platform for MSMEs to be created to enable filing of bills and payment thereof, to eliminate delays in government payments.

- India's first indigenously developed payment ecosystem for transport, based on National Common Mobility Card (NCMC) standards, launched in March 2019.

- Inter-operable transport card runs on RuPay card and would allow the holders to pay for bus travel, toll taxes, parking charges, retail shopping.

- Massive push given to all forms of physical connectivity through:

  - Pradhan Mantri Gram Sadak Yojana.

  - Industrial Corridors, Dedicated Freight Corridors.

  - Bhartamala and Sagarmala projects, Jal Marg Vikas and UDAN Schemes.

- State road networks to be developed in second phase of Bharatmala project.

- Navigational capacity of Ganga to be enhanced via multi modal terminals at Sahibganj and Haldia and a navigational lock at Farakka by 2019-20, under Jal Marg Vikas Project.

- Four times increase in next four years estimated in the cargo volume on Ganga, leading to cheaper freight and passenger movement and reducing the import bill.

- Rs. 50 lakh crore investment needed in Railway Infrastructure during 2018-2030.

- Public-Private-Partnership proposed for development and completion of tracks, rolling stock manufacturing and delivery of passenger freight services.

- 657 kilometers of Metro Rail network has become operational across the country.

- Policy interventions to be made for the development of Maintenance, Repair and Overhaul (MRO), to achieve self-reliance in aviation segment.

- Regulatory roadmap for making India a hub for aircraft financing and leasing activities from Indian shores, to be laid by the Government.

- Outlay of Rs. 10,000 crore for 3 years approved for Phase-II of FAME Scheme.

- Upfront incentive proposed on purchase and charging infrastructure, to encourage faster adoption of Electric Vehicles.

- Only advanced-battery-operated and registered e-vehicles to be incentivized under FAME Scheme.

- National Highway Programme to be restructured to ensure a National Highway Grid, using a financeable model.

- Power at affordable rates to states ensured under 'One Nation, One Grid'.

- Blueprints to be made available for gas grids, water grids, i-ways, and regional airports.

- High Level Empowered Committee (HLEC) recommendations to be implemented :

  > Retirement of old & inefficient plants.

  > Addressing low utilization of gas plant capacity due to paucity of Natural Gas.

- Cross subsidy surcharges, undesirable duties on open access sales or captive generation for industrial and other bulk power consumers to be removed under **Ujjwal DISCOM Assurance Yojana (UDAY).**

- Package of power sector tariff and structural reforms to be announced soon.

- Reform measures to be taken up to promote **rental housing.**

- **Model Tenancy Law** to be finalized and circulated to the states.

- *Joint development* and *concession* mechanisms to be used for public infrastructure and affordable housing on land parcels held by the Central Government and CPSEs.

- Measures to enhance the sources of capital for infrastructure financing:
  - ➢ Credit Guarantee Enhancement Corporation to be set up in 2019-2020.
  - ➢ Action plan to be put in place to deepen the market for long term bonds with focus on infrastructure.
  - ➢ Proposed transfer/sale of investments by FIIs/FPIs (in debt securities issued by IDF-NBFCs) to any domestic investor within the specified lock-in period.

❑ **Measures to deepen bond markets :**
  - Stock exchanges to be enabled to allow AA rated bonds as collaterals.
  - User-friendliness of trading platforms for corporate bonds to be reviewed.

❑ **Social stock exchange :**
  - Electronic fund raising platform under the regulatory ambit of SEBI.
  - Listing social enterprises and voluntary organizations.
  - To raise capital as equity, debt or as units like a mutual fund.
  - SEBI to consider raising the threshold for minimum public shareholding in the listed companies from 25% to 35%.
  - Know Your Customer (KYC) norms for Foreign Portfolio Investors to be made more investor friendly.
  - Government to supplement efforts by RBI to get retail investors to invest in government treasury bills and securities, with further institutional development using stock exchanges.
  - Measures to make India a more attractive FDI destination:
    - ➢ FDI in sectors like aviation, media (animation, AVGC) and insurance sectors can be opened further after multi-stakeholder examination.
    - ➢ Insurance Intermediaries to get 100% FDI.
    - ➢ Local sourcing norms to be eased for FDI in Single Brand Retail sector.

- Government to organize an annual Global Investors Meet in India, using National Infrastructure Investment Fund (NIIF) as an anchor to get all three sets of global players (pension, insurance and sovereign wealth funds).

- Statutory limit for FPI investment in a company is proposed to be increased from 24% to sectoral foreign investment limit. Option to be given to the concerned corporate to limit it to a lower threshold.

- FPIs to be permitted to subscribe to listed debt securities issued by ReITs and InvITs.

- NRI-Portfolio Investment Scheme Route is proposed to be merged with the Foreign Portfolio Investment Route.

- Cumulative resources garnered through new financial instruments like Infrastructure Investment Trusts (InvITs), Real Estate Investment Trusts (REITs) as well as models like Toll-Operate-Transfer (ToT) exceed Rs. 24,000 crore.

- **New Space India Limited (NSIL),** a PSE, incorporated as a new commercial arm of Department of Space.

- To tap the benefits of the Research & Development carried out by ISRO like commercialization of products like launch vehicles, transfer to technologies and marketing of space products.

❑ **Direct Taxes**

- Tax rate reduced to 25% for companies with annual turnover up to Rs. 400 crore

- Surcharge increased on individuals having taxable income from Rs. 2 crore to Rs. 5 crore and Rs. 5 crore and above.

- India's Ease of Doing Business ranking under the category of 'paying taxes' jumped from 172 in 2017 to 121 in the 2019.

- Direct tax revenue increased by over 78% in past 5 years to Rs. 11.37 lakh crore

❑ **Tax Simplification and Ease of living** - *making compliance easier by leveraging technology :*

● **Interchangeability of PAN and Aadhaar**

  ➢ Those who don't have PAN can file tax returns using Aadhaar.

  ➢ Aadhaar can be used wherever PAN is required.

● **Pre-filling of Income-tax Returns** for faster, more accurate tax returns

  ➢ Pre-filled tax returns with details of several incomes and deductions to be made available.

  ➢ Information to be collected from Banks, Stock exchanges, mutual funds etc.

● **Faceless e-assessment**

  ➢ Faceless e-assessment with no human interface to be launched.

  ➢ To be carried out initially in cases requiring verification of certain specified transactions or discrepancies.

● **Affordable housing**

  ➢ Additional deduction up to Rs. 1.5 lakhs for interest paid on loans borrowed up to 31st March, 2020 for purchase of house valued up to Rs. 45 lakh.

  ➢ Overall benefit of around Rs. 7 lakh over loan period of 15 years.

● **Boost to Electric Vehicles**

  ➢ Additional income tax deduction of Rs. 1.5 lakh on interest paid on electric vehicle loans.

  ➢ Customs duty exempted on certain parts of electric vehicles.

❑ **Other Direct Tax measures**

● *Simplification of tax laws to reduce genuine hardships of taxpayers :*

- ➢ Higher tax threshold for launching prosecution for non-filing of returns

- ➢ Appropriate class of persons exempted from the anti-abuse provisions of Section 50CA and Section 56 of the Income Tax Act.

❑ **Relief for Start-ups**

- Capital gains exemptions from sale of residential house for investment in start-ups extended till FY21.

- 'Angel tax' issue resolved- start-ups and investors filing requisite declarations and providing information in their returns not to be subjected to any kind of scrutiny in respect of valuations of share premiums.

- Funds raised by start-ups to not require scrutiny from Income Tax Department

  - ➢ E-verification mechanism for establishing identity of the investor and source of funds.

- Special administrative arrangements for pending assessments and grievance redressal

  - ➢ No inquiry in such cases by the Assessing Officer without obtaining approval of the supervisory officer.

- No scrutiny of valuation of shares issued to Category-II Alternative Investment Funds.

- Relaxation of conditions for carry forward and set off of losses.

❑ **NBFCs**

- Interest on certain bad or doubtful debts by deposit taking as well as systemically important non-deposit taking NBFCs to be taxed in the year in which interest is actually received.

❑ **International Financial Services Centre (IFSC)**

- **Direct tax incentives proposed for an IFSC :**

  - ➢ 100 % profit-linked deduction in any ten-year block within a fifteen-year period.

> ➢ Exemption from dividend distribution tax from current and accumulated income to companies and mutual funds.

> ➢ Exemptions on capital gain to Category-III Alternative Investment Funds (AIFs).

> ➢ Exemption to interest payment on loan taken from non-residents.

❑ **Securities Transaction Tax (STT)**

- STT restricted only to the difference between settlement and strike price in case of exercise of options.

❑ **Indirect Taxes**

- Make In India

- Basic Customs Duty increased on cashew kernels, PVC, tiles, auto parts, marble slabs, optical fibre cable, CCTV camera etc.

- Exemptions from Custom Duty on certain electronic items now manufactured in India withdrawn.

- End use based exemptions on palm stearin, fatty oils withdrawn.

- Exemptions to various kinds of papers withdrawn.

- 5% Basic Custom Duty imposed on imported books.

- Customs duty reduced on certain raw materials such as:

  > ➢ Inputs for artificial kidney and disposable sterilised dialyser and fuels for nuclear power plants etc.

  > ➢ Capital goods required for manufacture of specified electronic goods.

❑ **Defence**

- Defence equipment not manufactured in India exempted from basic customs duty

❑ **Other Indirect Tax provisions**

- Export duty rationalised on raw and semi-finished leather

- Increase in Special Additional Excise Duty and Road and Infrastructure Cess each by Rs. 1 per litre on petrol and diesel

- Custom duty on gold and other precious metals increased
- Legacy Dispute Resolution Scheme for quick closure of pending litigations in Central Excise and Service tax from pre-GST regime

❑ **Grameen Bharat / Rural India**

- **Ujjwala** Yojana and **Saubhagya** Yojana have transformed the lives of every rural family, dramatically improving ease of their living.

- Electricity and clean cooking facility to all willing rural families by 2022.

- **Pradhan Mantri Awas Yojana –** *Gramin (PMAY-G) aims to achieve "Housing for All" by 2022* :

  ➢ Eligible beneficiaries to be provided 1.95 crore houses with amenities like toilets, electricity and LPG connections during its second phase (2019-20 to 2021-22).

- **Pradhan Mantri Matsya Sampada Yojana (PMMSY)**

  ➢ A robust fisheries management framework through PMMSY to be established by the Department of Fisheries.

  ➢ To address critical gaps in the value chain including infrastructure, modernization, traceability, production, productivity, post-harvest management, and quality control.

- **Pradhan Mantri Gram Sadak Yojana (PMGSY)**

  ➢ Target of connecting the eligible and feasible habitations advanced from 2022 to 2019 with 97% of such habitations already being provided with all weather connectivity.

  ➢ 30,000 kilometers of PMGSY roads have been built using Green Technology, Waste Plastic and Cold Mix Technology, thereby reducing carbon footprint.

  ➢ 1,25,000 kilometers of road length to be upgraded over the next five years under PMGSY III with an estimated cost of Rs. 80,250 crore.

- **Scheme of Fund for Upgradation and Regeneration of Traditional Industries' (SFURTI)**
  - ➢ Common Facility Centres (CFCs) to be setup to facilitate cluster based development for making traditional industries more productive, profitable and capable for generating sustained employment opportunities.
  - ➢ 100 new clusters to be setup during 2019-20 with special focus on Bamboo, Honey and Khadi, enabling 50,000 artisans to join the economic value chain.

- **Scheme for Promotion of Innovation, Rural Industry and Entrepreneurship' (ASPIRE)** consolidated.
  - ➢ 80 Livelihood Business Incubators (LBIs) and 20 Technology Business Incubators (TBIs) to be setup in 2019-20.
  - ➢ 75,000 entrepreneurs to be skilled in agro-rural industry sectors.

- Private entrepreneurships to be supported in driving value-addition to farmers' produce from the field and for those from allied activities.

- Dairying through cooperatives to be encouraged by creating infrastructure for cattle feed manufacturing, milk procurement, processing & marketing.

- 10,000 new Farmer Producer Organizations to be formed, to ensure economies of scale for farmers.

- Government to work with State Governments to allow farmers to benefit from e-NAM.

- Zero Budget Farming in which few states' farmers are already being trained to be replicated in other states.

- **India's water security**
  - ➢ New Jal Shakti Mantralaya to look at the management of our water resources and water supply in an integrated and holistic manner
  - ➢ Jal Jeevan Mission to achieve Har Ghar Jal (piped water supply) to all rural households by 2024

> To focus on integrated demand and supply side management of water at the local level.

> Convergence with other Central and State Government Schemes to achieve its objectives.

> 1592 critical and over exploited Blocks spread across 256 District being identified for the Jal Shakti Abhiyan.

> Compensatory Afforestation Fund Management and Planning Authority (CAMPA) fund can be used for this purpose.

- **Swachh Bharat Abhiyan**

  > 9.6 crore toilets constructed since Oct 2, 2014.

  > More than 5.6 lakh villages have become Open Defecation Free (ODF).

  > Swachh Bharat Mission to be expanded to undertake sustainable solid waste management in every village.

- **Pradhan Mantri Gramin Digital Saksharta Abhiyan,**

  > Over two crore rural Indians made digitally literate.

  > Internet connectivity in local bodies in every Panchayat under Bharat-Net to bridge rural-urban divide.

  > Universal Obligation Fund under a PPP arrangement to be utilized for speeding up Bharat-Net.

❑ **Shahree Bharat/Urban India**

- Pradhan Mantri Awas Yojana – Urban (PMAY-Urban)-

  > Over 81 lakh houses with an investment of about Rs. 4.83 lakh crore sanctioned of which construction started in about 47 lakh houses.

  > Over 26 lakh houses completed of which nearly 24 lakh houses delivered to the beneficiaries.

  > Over 13 lakh houses so far constructed using new technologies.

- More than 95% of cities also declared Open Defecation Free (ODF).

- Almost 1 crore citizens have downloaded Swachhata App.
- Target of achieving Gandhiji's resolve of Swachh Bharat to make India ODF by 2nd October 2019.
  - ➤ To mark this occasion, the Rashtriya Swachhta Kendra to be inaugurated at Gandhi Darshan, Rajghat on 2nd October, 2019.

❑ **Gandhipedia** being developed by National Council for Science Museums to sensitize youth and society about positive Gandhian values.

- Railways to be encouraged to invest more in suburban railways through SPV structures like Rapid Regional Transport System (RRTS) proposed on the Delhi-Meerut route.
- *Proposal to enhance the metro-railway initiatives by* :
  - ➤ Encouraging more PPP initiatives.
  - ➤ Ensuring completion of sanctioned works.
  - ➤ Supporting transit oriented development (TOD) to ensure commercial activity around transit hubs.

❑ **Youth**

- New National Education Policy to be brought which proposes
  - ➤ Major changes in both school and higher education
  - ➤ Better Governance systems
  - ➤ Greater focus on research and innovation.

❑ **National Research Foundation (NRF)** proposed

To fund, coordinate and promote research in the country.

To assimilate independent research grants given by various Ministries.

To strengthen overall research eco-system in the country

This would be adequately supp lemented with additional funds.

- Rs. 400 crore provided for "World Class Institutions", for FY 2019-20, more than three times the revised estimates for the previous year.

- **'Study in India'** proposed to bring foreign students to study in Indian higher educational institutions.

- Regulatory systems of higher education to be reformed comprehensively :

  - ➢ To promote greater autonomy.

  - ➢ To focus on better academic outcomes.

- Draft legislation to set up **Higher Education Commission of India (HECI)**, to be presented.

- **Khelo India Scheme** to be expanded with all necessary financial support.

- **National Sports Education Board** for development of sportspersons to be set up under Khelo India, to popularize sports at all levels

- To prepare youth for overseas jobs, focus to be increased on globally valued skill-sets including language training, AI, IoT, Big Data, 3D Printing, Virtual Reality and Robotics.

- Set of four labour codes proposed, to streamline multiple labour laws to standardize and streamline registration and filing of returns.

- A television program proposed exclusively for and by start-ups, within the DD bouquet of channels.

- Stand-Up India Scheme to be continued for the period of 2020-25. The Banks to provide financial assistance for demand based businesses.

❑ **Ease of Living**

- About 30 lakh workers joined the Pradhan Mantri Shram Yogi Maandhan Scheme that provides Rs. 3,000 per month as pension on attaining the age of 60 to workers in unorganized and informal sectors.

- Approximately 35 crore LED bulbs distributed under UJALA Yojana leading to cost saving of Rs. 18,341 crore annually.

- Solar stoves and battery chargers to be promoted using the approach of LED bulbs mission.

- A massive program of railway station modernization to be launched.

❑ **Naari Tu Narayani/Women**

- Approach shift from women-centric-policy making to women-led initiatives and movements.

- A Committee proposed with Government and private stakeholders for moving forward on Gender budgeting.

- **SHG :**

  ➢ Women SHG interest subvention program proposed to be expanded to all districts.

  ➢ Overdraft of Rs. 5,000 to be allowed for every verified women SHG member having a Jan Dhan Bank Account.

  ➢ One woman per SHG to be eligible for a loan up to Rs. 1 lakh under MUDRA Scheme.

❑ **India's Soft Power**

- Proposal to consider issuing Aadhaar Card for NRIs with Indian Passports on their arrival without waiting for 180 days.

- Mission to integrate traditional artisans with global markets proposed, with necessary patents and geographical indicators.

- 18 new Indian diplomatic Missions in Africa approved in March, 2018, out of which 5 already opened. Another 4 new Embassies intended in 2019-20.

- Revamp of Indian Development Assistance Scheme (IDEAS) proposed.

- 17 iconic Tourism Sites being developed into model world class tourist destinations.

- Present digital repository aimed at preserving rich tribal cultural heritage, to be strengthened.

❑ **Banking and Financial Sector**

- NPAs of commercial banks reduced by over Rs. 1 lakh crore over the last year.

- Record recovery of over Rs. 4 lakh crore effected over the last four years.

- Provision coverage ratio at its highest in seven years.
- Domestic credit growth increased to 13.8%.

❑ **Measures related to PSBs :**

➢ Rs. 70,000 crore proposed to be provided to PSBs to boost credit.

➢ PSBs to leverage technology, offering online personal loans and doorstep banking, and enabling customers of one PSBs to access services across all PSBs.

➢ Steps to be initiated to empower accountholders to have control over deposit of cash by others in their accounts.

➢ Reforms to be undertaken to strengthen governance in PSBs.

❑ **Measures related to NBFCs :**

- Proposals for strengthening the regulatory authority of RBI over NBFCs to be placed in the Finance Bill.

- Requirement of creating a Debenture Redemption Reserve will be done away with to allow NBFCs to raise funds in public issues.

- Steps to allow all NBFCs to directly participate on the TReDS platform.

- Return of regulatory authority from NHB to RBI proposed, over the housing finance sector.

- Rs. 100 lakh crore investment in infrastructure intended over the next five years. Committee proposed to recommend the structure and required flow of funds through development finance institutions.

- Steps to be taken to separate the NPS Trust from PFRDA.

- Reduction in Net Owned Fund requirement from Rs. 5,000 crore to Rs. 1,000 crore proposed :

  ➢ To facilitate on-shoring of international insurance transactions.

  ➢ To enable opening of branches by foreign reinsurers in the International Financial Services Centre.

❏ **Measures related to CPSEs :**

- Target of Rs. 1, 05,000 crore of disinvestment receipts set for the FY 2019-20.

- Government to reinitiate the process of strategic disinvestment of Air India, and to offer more CPSEs for strategic participation by the private sector.

- Government to undertake strategic sale of PSUs and continue to consolidate PSUs in the non-financial space.

- Government to consider going to an appropriate level below 51% in PSUs where the government control is still to be retained, on case to case basis.

- Present policy of retaining 51% Government stake to be modified to retaining 51% stake inclusive of the stake of Government controlled institutions.

- Retail participation in CPSEs to be encouraged.

- To provide additional investment space:

  ➢ Government to realign its holding in CPSEs

  ➢ Banks to permit greater availability of its shares and to improve depth of its market.

- Government to offer an investment option in ETFs on the lines of Equity Linked Savings Scheme (ELSS).

  ➢ Government to meet public shareholding norms of 25% for all listed PSUs and raise the foreign shareholding limits to maximum permissible sector limits for all PSU companies which are part of Emerging Market Index.

- Government to raise a part of its gross borrowing program in external markets in external currencies. This will also have beneficial impact on demand situation for the government securities in domestic market.

- New series of coins of One Rupee, Two Rupees, Five Rupees, Ten Rupees and Twenty Rupees, easily identifiable to the visually impaired to be made available for public use shortly.

❑ **Digital Payments**

- TDS of 2% on cash withdrawal exceeding Rs. 1 crore in a year from a bank account

- Business establishments with annual turnover more than Rs. 50 crore shall offer low cost digital modes of payment to their customers and no charges or Merchant Discount Rate shall be imposed on customers as well as merchants.

❑ **Mega Investment in Sunrise and Advanced Technology Areas**

- Scheme to invite global companies to set up mega manufacturing plants in areas such as Semi-conductor Fabrication (FAB), Solar Photo Voltaic cells, Lithium storage batteries, Computer Servers, Laptops, etc

  ➢ Investment linked income tax exemptions to be provided along with indirect tax benefits.

❑ **Achievements during 2014-19**

- 1 trillion dollar added to Indian economy over last 5 years (compared to over 55 years taken to reach the first tril lion dollar).

- India is now the 6th largest economy in the world, compared to 11th largest five years ago.

- Indian economy is globally the 3rd largest in Purchasing Power Parity (PPP) terms.

- Strident commitment to fiscal discipline and a rejuvenated Centre-State dynamic provided during 2014-19.

- Structural reforms in indirect taxation, bankruptcy and real estate carried out.

- Average amount spent on food security per year almost doubled during 2014-19 compared to 2009-14.

- Patents issued more than trebled in 2017-18 as against the number in 2014.

- Ball set rolling for a New India, planned and assisted by the NITI Aayog.

❑ **Roadmap for future**

- Simplification of procedures.

- Incentivizing performance.

- Red-tape reduction.

- Making the best use of technology.

- Accelerating mega programmes and services initiated and delivered so far.

Economic Current Affairs

❑ **Steps Ahead For the Cashless Economy**

GST council and recommendation on 21ˢᵗ July 2018:

The Customers who are using BHIM and RUPAY Card for the payment, they will get the rebate of 20% to 100 rupees maximum on all Goods and Services, this service will be in the form of Cash-back and will be deposited directly in the users Bank Account.

Note:

- Presently, the numbers of Users of RUPAY Cardholders are Twenty Eight Crore in which twenty-four Crore are JANDHAN Account holders and a large number of people who have KISAN Card are also using RUPAY CARD.

- This facility will not be provided to those who are having VISA Card and MASTER Card.

- In this Project implementation, the Government has to bear One thousand Crore on Yearly Basis this will create a huge burden on government but in terms of future benefit situation will be on the Government side. The implementation of this project will also be increasing the range of digital transaction, transparency and will decrease the transaction of Black Money in the organized sector, eventually; the Government's revenue will grow.

- The BHIM App was developed by National Payment Corporation of India (NPCI) and launched on 30th December 2016.

Steps taken in December 2017:

- The MDR on Debit Card users for making a payment of the rupees up to 2000 would be paid by Government itself for two years that means the bank will not be charging the amount from the Debit Card Users. (The MDR is the fee that the store accepting your card has to pay to the bank when you swipe it for payments).

- The same facility would also be given to online payments for Insurance Policy, Rail Tickets, and Highways Toll Taxes.

Steps taken in December 2016:

- The Digital Cash back facility on Petrol Pumps for the customers of Debit/Credit Card Holders was revised from 0.75 per cent to 0.25 per cent. The amount had to be deposited directly to the customer's bank account.

Benefits of Cashless Economy:

- This helps to curb corruption.

- The flow of black money which results in an increase of economic growth.

- The transparency in the financial system

- It leads to lesser funding for illegal trades and activities including terrorism.

- It increase the liquidity in Banks and decrease the Interest Rate and the lowest interest rate eventually increase the "Entrepreneurship" which lead to the new investments and economic development through job creation.

- The Notes printing cost increase the Government's Expenditure and also effects negatively to Nature.

Challenges in the way of Cashless Economy:

- More than 60% of Indian population belongs to rural region they are not comfortable using computers or mobile phones for transactions.

- Security is another big concern regarding cashless transactions.

- The limitations of quality internet access.

❑ **Indian economy – Global Evaluation**

S.N.	Country	GDP in Trillions
1.	USA	19.39
2.	China	12.33
3.	Japan	4.87
4.	Germany	3.67
5.	Britain	2.62
6.	India	2.59
7.	France	2.58
8.	Brazil	2.05
9.	Italy	1.93
10.	Canada	1.65

Top Largest countries on the basis of population

Ten Countries with the Highest Population in the World are:

S.No.	Countries
1.	China
2.	India
3.	United States
4.	Indonesia
5.	Brazil
6.	Pakistan
7.	Nigeria
8.	Bangladesh
9.	Russia
10.	Mexico

Important Facts:

- The World Population Prospects: The 2017 Revision, published by the UN Department of Economic and Social Affairs, provides a comprehensive review of global demographic trends and prospects for the future,

- The new projections include some notable findings at the country level. China (with 1.4 billion inhabitants) and India (1.3 billion inhabitants) comprising 19 and 18% of the total global population. In roughly seven years, or around 2024, the population of India is expected to surpass that of China.

❑ **GST: Global Evaluation**

- The World Bank said in a report The goods and services tax (GST) implemented by government of India from 1 July 2017 is one of the most highest tax rate in the world among a sample of 115 countries which have a similar indirect tax system.

- World's highest GST rate is implementing by Chile which is situated in South America.

GST rates implementing by famous countries are:

S.No.	Countries	GST Rates in percents (%)
1	Malaysia	6
2	Singapore , Thailand	7
3	Australia , Indonesia	10
4	South Africa	14
5	New Zealand , Mauritius	15
6	Germany	19
7	Britain	20
8	Denmark	25

- According to the World Bank's biannual India Development Update report, most countries in the world have a single rate of GST: "49 countries use a single rate, 28 use two rates and only five countries including India use four rates,"

- The countries that use four or more slabs of GST include Italy, Luxembourg, Pakistan and Ghana. Thus, India has among the highest number of different GST slabs in the world.

Tax Rates	Products
0%	Hulled cereal grains like barley, wheat, oat, rye, etc., Bones and horn cores unworked and waste of these products., Palmyra jiggery, All types of salt, Picture books, colouring books or drawing books for children Human hair – dressed, thinned, bleached or otherwise worked Sanitary Napkins
5%	Household necessities such as edible oil, sugar, spices, tea, and coffee (except instant) are included. Coal , Mishti/Mithai (Indian Sweets) and Life-saving drugs are also covered under this GST slab
12%	This includes computers and processed food
18%	Hair oil, toothpaste and soaps, capital goods and industrialintermediaries are covered in this slab
28%	Luxury items such as small cars, consumer durables like AC and Refrigerators, premium cars, cigarettes and aerated drinks, High-end motorcycles are included here.

- Nearly 81 per cent of the items fall under below-18 per cent GST rate slabs. And all the Luxury items or only 19 per cent of the goods comes under the 28 percent of tax slabs.

- the Indian system of indirect taxation there were 17 Taxes & and 23 Cesses of Central and State taxes, by amalgamating a large number of taxes Good and Service Tax has been enable in India.

- In short, GST replaces most of indirect taxes to create a Single Tax System, Uniform across the Country making entire Nation as a Single Market. That is One Nation – One Tax – One Market.

❑ **Prompt Corrective Actions**

Meaning of PCA: PCA norms allow the regulator to place certain restrictions such as halting branch expansion and stopping dividend payment. It can even cap a bank's lending limit to one entity or sector. Other corrective actions that can be imposed on banks include special audit, restructuring operations and activation of recovery plan. Banks' promoters can be asked to bring in new management, too. The RBI can also supersede the bank's board, under PCA.

Note: Reserve Bank of India (RBI) issued a Prompt Corrective Action (PCA) framework to maintain sound financial health of banks. It facilitates banks in breach of risk thresholds for identified areas of monitoring, *viz.,* capital, asset quality (which is tracked in terms of the net Non-Performing Assets ratio) and profitability, to take corrective measures in a timely manner, in order to restore their financial health. Thus, it is intended to encourage banks to eschew certain riskier activities, improve operational efficiency and focus on conserving capital to strengthen them. The framework is not intended to constrain the performance of normal operations of the banks for the general public. RBI has placed eleven PSBs, *viz.,* Dena Bank, Central Bank of India, Bank of Maharashtra, UCO Bank, IDBI Bank, and Oriental Bank of Commerce, Indian Overseas Bank, Corporation Bank, Bank of India, Allahabad Bank and United Bank of India under the PCA framework.

Narrow banking is also called a safe bank. Narrow banking would restrict banks to holding liquid and safe government bonds. Loans would be made by other financial intermediaries.

❑ **Directorate General of trade remedies**

• The Government of India carried out an Amendment to the Government of India (Allocation of Business) Rules, 1961 substituting "Directorate General of Trade Remedies" in place of "Directorate General of Anti-Dumping and Allied Duties" in Department of Commerce.

- This has paved way for creation of an integrated single umbrella National Authority to be called the Directorate General of Trade Remedies (DGTR) for providing comprehensive and swift trade defence mechanism in India.

- The amendment of Allocation of Business Rules has also mandated Department of Commerce with work pertaining to recommendation of Safeguard measures.

❑ **Foreign Direct Investment (Updates)**

Foreign Direct Investment (FDI) is a major driver of economic growth and a source of non-debt finance for the economic development of the country.

Year	FDI (In Billion Dollar)
2016-17	60
2017-18	61.96

India's topmost attractive sectors for foreign direct investment-

1. Service
2. Computer Software and Hardware
3. Telecom
4. Manufracture
5. Trading
6. Automotive

The largest source of foreign investment in India –

1. Mauritius
2. Singapore
3. Japan
4. Netherlands
5. USA
6. Germany

❑ **India raised the duties on US Goods**

- India has hiked customs duty on 29 products several goods, 25 per cent and 10 per cent duty on steel and aluminum respectively, including pulses and iron, imported from the US as a retaliatory action against the tariff hike by Washington, a move that has sparked fears of a global trade war, "A situation in which countries try to damage each other's trade, typically by the imposition of tariffs or quota restrictions".

- India had submitted to the WTO a list of 30 items on which it proposed to raise customs duty in the notification products are , — such as apples, walnuts, almonds, high-end motorcycles (including Harley Davidson), lentils and phosphoric acid — on which duties are likely to be raised by 10-50 per cent.

Important Facts

- India is the latest major economy to hit back against US President Donald Trump's tariff hikes on steel and aluminium,it has taken the step against the Protection Policy of America and imposing the High Tariff Duty on its products.

- India had asked the US government to exempt it from the 25% steel tariff and 10% aluminium tariff imposed by Trump on grounds of national security. The US rejected India's request so , it is the tit-for-tat action of India against the USA. India has also dragged the US to the dispute settlement mechanism in the WTO over the matter.

❑ **Project Sashakt**

Announced on   - 4th July 2018

Objective   - a five-pronged strategy to resolve bad loans,

Ministry   - Ministry of Finance

Important Fact   - Project Sashakt was proposed by a panel led by PNB chairman Sunil Mehta.

It is the five-pronged strategy to deal with non-performing assets (NPAs) recommended by the Sunil Mehta-led committee.

Category	Formula
To deal with NPA of Up to 50 Crore	For loans up to Rs. 50 crore, the panel has suggested a steering committee within the bank to resolve it within 90 days.
To deal with NPA of Up to 50 to 500 Crores	For bad loans of Rs. 50-500 crore, banks will enter an inter-creditor agreement, authorizing the lead bank to implement a resolution plan in 180 days.

To deal with NPA of Up to 500 Crores	For loans above Rs. 500 crore, the panel recom-mended an independent AMC, supported by institutional funding through the AIF. The idea is to help consolidate stressed assets.

Asset Management Company : For loans above Rs. 500 crore, an independent asset management company (AMC) will be set up. Project Sashakt is to ensure the operational turnaround of the banks and stressed companies so that the asset value is retained. The resolution process suggested by the committee will also help bring in credible long-term external capital to limit the burden on the domestic banking sector while ensuring robust governance and credit architecture to prevent a similar build-up of non-performing loans in the future; an alternative investment fund (AIF) would raise funds from institutional investors. Banks would be given an option to invest in this fund if they wish. AIFs can also bid for assets in NCLT. The lead bank can discover price discovery through the open auction route. Security receipts have to be redeemed within 60 days.

❑ **Public Credit Registry**

The concept of Public Credit Registry and its objective: On the recommendations of a committee, headed by Y.M. Deosthalee , a public credit registry has been set up it works as an information repository that collates all loan information of individuals and corporate borrowers. A credit repository will help banks distinguish between a bad and a good borrower and accordingly offer attractive interest rates to good borrowers and higher interest rates to bad borrowers.

A PCR will help in a) Credit assessment and pricing by banks; b) Risk-based, dynamic and countercyclical provisioning at banks; c) Supervision and early intervention by regulators; d) Understanding if transmission of monetary policy is working, and if not, where are the bottlenecks; and, e) How to restructure stressed bank credits effectively.

Main Provision of PCR : A comprehensive credit information repository covering all types of credit facilities (funded and non-funded) extended by all credit institutions – commercial banks, cooperative banks, NBFCs, MFIs – and also covering borrowings from other sources, including external commercial borrowing and borrowings from market, is essential to ascertain the total indebtedness of a legal or natural person.

❑ **Atal Tinkering Labs**

The government think tank NITI Aayog has reportedly **given permission to 3,000 additional schools** to set up Atal Tinkering Labs under its Atal Innovation Mission (AIM)

The objective of this scheme is to foster curiosity, creativity and imagination in young minds and inculcate skills such as design mind - set , computational thinking, adaptive learning, physical computing, rapid calculations, measurements etc. Young children will get a chance to work with tools and equipment to understand what, how and why aspects of STEM (Science, Technology, Engineering and Math).

This will bring the total number schools with Atal Tinkering Labs to **5,441.** "The selected schools shall receive a grant of INR 20 lakh spread over the next five years to establish Atal Tinkering Labs for nurturing innovation and entrepreneurial spirit among secondary school children across India," NITI Aayog said in a media statement. It will facilitate the creation of over one million neoteric child innovators by 2020.

❑ **Umang App**

Launched By :- Employees' Provident Fund Organisation (EPFO)

Functions:- EPFO members can link their UAN with Aadhaar , for using this facility with UMANG APP, Member will have to provide his/her UAN. An OTP will be sent to the UAN registered Mobile Number. After OTP Verification, member will have to provide Aadhaar details and gender information (where gender information is not available against UAN). Another OTP will be sent on Aadhaar Registered Mobile Number and/or email. After OTP verification, Aadhaar will be linked with UAN where UAN and Aadhaar details are matched.

UMANG app is a common platform for various government services such as gas booking, Aadhaar, crop insurance, EPF and National Pension System. The app was launched with the provisions of 43 government departments that grants access to 150+ services and has a target to reach 200 departments granting access to 1200+ services by December 2019.

If one has applied for the PAN card, they can also check the status of the application using this app. Pensioners can generate their digital life certificate using this app. If you have an NPS (National Pension System) account, you can check your current holdings, account details, recent contributions using UMANG app.One can also apply for a change in the address some of the services using this app and can change the schemes under NPS using this app. Job seekers can also register themselves under the Pradhan Mantri Kaushal Vikas Yojana using UMANG app.

❑ **Digital India Interneship scheme**

Launched By : The Union Ministry of Electronics and Information Technology (MeITY) has launched the website of Digital India Internship Scheme.

Purpose: An internship is an opportunity for a student to secure first hand and practical work experience under the guidance of a qualified and experienced Supervisor/Mentor. It also aims at active participation in the learning process through experimentation and putting into practice the knowledge acquired in the classrooms.

Eligibility :

(i) Indian students from recognized universities in India who have secured at least 60% marks in the last held degree or certificate examination and:-

    (a) Pursuing B.Tech/B.E., and are in the 2nd/3rd year of the 10+2+4 pattern of education

OR

    (b) Pursuing integrated degree course or dual degree (B.E./ B.Tech, M.E./M.Tech.) and are in the 4th/5th year of the 10+2+5 pattern of education.

(ii) Possessing minimum qualifications as above shall not guarantee internship in this Ministry. Candidates having exposure in the area of intended internship with good academic background and having higher qualification, based on need shall be given preference.

Duration of Internship :

Internship would be offered two times in a year i.e. summer Internship during May and June and winter Internship during December and January.

No. of Selected Students : 25

❑ **Ease of Doing Business Index 2018**

Date : 10 July 2018

Released by : Department of Industrial Policy and Promotion (DIPP), Ministry of Commerce   and Industry,

Meaning of Ease of Doing Business : It is an aggregate figure that includes different parameters which define the ease of doing business in a state.

States in Ease of Doing Business :   1. Andhra Pradesh, 2. Telangana, 3. Haryana, 4. Jharkhand 5. Gujarat, 6. Chhatisgarh, 7. Madhya Pradesh, 8. Rajasthan, 10. West Bengal.

Note : UP is on the 12th position.

Important Facts : The current assessment under the BRAP 2017 is based on a combined score consisting of **Reform evidence score** that is based on evidences uploaded by the States and UTs and **Feedback score** that is based on the feedback garnered from the actual users of the services provided to the businesses.

States and UTs have conducted reforms to ease their regulations and systems in areas such as labour, environmental clearances, single window system, construction permits, contract enforcement, registering property and inspections. States and UTs have also enacted Public Service Delivery Guarantee Act to enforce the timelines on registrations and approvals.

The Assam, Bihar, and Himachal Pradesh, states have improved their score in "ease of doing business index."

❑ **Zero Budget Natural Farming – ZBNF**

Meaning of ZNBF:- Zero Budget Natural Farming (ZBNF) is a set of farming methods, and also a grassroots peasant movement, which has spread to various states in India. It has attained wide success in southern India, especially the southern Indian state of Karnataka where it first evolved. The movement in Karnataka state was born out of collaboration between Mr Subhash Palekar, who put together the ZBNF practices, and the state farmers association Karnataka Rajya Raitha Sangha (KRRS). The word 'budget' refers to credit and expenses, thus the phrase 'Zero Budget' means without using any credit, and without spending any money on purchased inputs. 'Natural farming' means farming with Nature and without chemicals. This means that farmers need not purchase fertilizers and pesticides in order to ensure the healthy growth of crops. Farmers use earthworms, cow dung, urine, plants, human excreta and such biological fertilizers for crop protection.

Causes of Adopting ZBNF

Indian farmers increasingly find themselves in a vicious cycle of debt, because of the high production costs, high interest rates for credit, the volatile market prices of crops, the rising costs of fossil fuel based inputs, and private seeds. Therefore, they choose suicide. Debt is like a leech for farmers of all sizes in India. Under such conditions, 'zero budget natural farming promises to end a reliance on loans and drastically cuts production costs , ending the debt cycle for desperate farmers. 'Natural farming' means farming with Nature and without chemicals, which conserves biodiversity and nurtures the balance. It not only, decreases oil erosion but also makes the soil breathe again. It enriches the soil with nutrients. it protects us from the harmful chemicals, as well as the curses such as cancer, diabetes and man y others, by not using any slow – poisoning pesticides , herbicides or fertilizers which with time incorporates into the human body, that is, biomagnifications.

Smaller farmers who took loans to afford the necessary input costs in terms of pesticides, fertilizers, pump sets etc. would often end up embroiled in debt if the crop failed. The agricultural sector also began a largely disorganized attempt to move from subsistence farming to cash cropping, which created its own set of problems. And lately, climate change and extreme weather events have only added to the havoc. According to the Global Climate Risk Index, India is one of three countries affected the most by extreme weather and happening series of natural disasters and ever increasing input costs is forcing Indian farmers towards suicidal attempts. he net result is a deadly combination of debt, crop failures, suicides, poverty and migration to urban areas that have drastically curtailed the quality of rural lives. For example, though 55-60% of India's workforce is engaged in agriculture, it contributes only 14% of India's GDP. India's GDP grew by 7.2% in 2014-15, but agriculture grew by 0.23% [at 2011-12 prices], and food grain production fell by 5%.

National Crime Records Bureau records show that at least, 284,694 Indian farmers have taken their lives since 1995. That means on average, a farmer has committed suicide every 30 minutes.

Benefits of Zero Budget Natural Farming:

In short, ZBNF is undoubtedly, economically, socially, biologically and physiologically a profound technique.

ZBNF involves methods that require no cost input from the farmer's side in terms of pesticides, fertilizers or even irrigation.

Natural methods are used to retain and improve soil health, control pests and increase yields. A farmer will also be able to produce his own seed and natural fertilizers are created using cow dung, cow urine and other materials. There was not a single example of farmers practicing zero-budget farming committing suicide, due to higher yield and low cost input.

In ZBNF, yields of various cash and food crops have been found to be significantly higher.E.g. yields from ZBNF plots were found on average to be 11% higher for cotton than in non-ZBNF plots.

Govt.'s initiative: Government of India has been promoting organic farming in the country through the dedicated schemes of Paramparagat Krishi Vikas Yojana (PKVY) since 2015-16 and also through Rashtriya Krishi Vikas Yojana (RKVY). In the revised guidelines of PKVY scheme during the year 2018, various organic farming models like Natural Farming, Rishi Farming, Vedic Farming, Cow Farming, Homa Farming, Zero Budget Natural Farming (ZBNF) etc. have been included wherein flexibility is given to states to adopt any model of Organic Farming including ZBNF depending on farmer's choice. Under the RKVY scheme, organic farming/ natural farming project components are considered by the respective State Level Sanctioning Committee (SLSC) according to their priority/ choice.

❑ **Inward Remittance in India**

Receipt of foreign exchange in India is called Inward remittance. Apart from exports there are other transactions, which generate inward remittance. For example Non-resident Indian staying abroad may remit foreign exchange to their relatives in India. A majority of remittances to India comes from Indian citizens living in the Gulf region.

The Reserve Bank released the results of its survey on India's inward remittances in 2016-17, the fourth in the series, It captures various aspects relating to remittances – source; destination; purpose of inward remittances; size; prevalent mode of transmission; and receivers'/ senders' cost of remittances. Responses were received from 42 major authorised dealers (ADs), accounting for 98.3 per cent of total remittances in 2016-17. A separate questionnaire was circulated among three major Money Transfer Operators (MTOs) that have large remittance operations in India.

Highlights

- Remittances to India were mostly routed through private sector banks (74.2 per cent), followed by public sector banks (17.3 per cent) and foreign banks (8.5 per cent).

- 82 per cent of the total remittances received by India originated from eight countries, viz., the United Arab Emirates, the United States, Saudi Arabia, Qatar, Kuwait, Oman, the United Kingdom and Malaysia.

- Kerala, Maharashtra, Karnataka and Tamil Nadu together received 58.7 per cent of total remittances.

- The rupee drawing arrangement (RDA) is the most popular channel of remittances which accounts for 75.2 per cent of remittances, followed by SWIFT (19.5 per cent), direct transfers (3.4 per cent) and cheques and drafts (1.9 per cent).

- Size-wise analysis shows that 70.3 per cent of all reported transactions were of more than US\$ 500 and only 2.7 per cent were of less than US\$ 200.

- More than half of remittances received by Indian residents were used for family maintenance, i.e., consumption (59.2 per cent), followed by deposits in banks (20 per cent) and investments in landed property and shares (8.3 per cent).

- Cost to the remitter for sending remittances through RDA is relatively low in the case of private /foreign banks

- The cost of receiving remittances through the RDA route is lowest in the case of public sector banks .

- MTOs operate mostly in the cash-to-cash services segment which accounts for 96.8 per cent of the total remittances routed through them.

- The cost of sending remittances through MTOs using the cash mode varies between 0.6 to 11.1 per cent, depending upon the size of remittances.

Table 1: Bank-wise Distribution of Inward Remittances

Per cent

Bank Group	Share in Total Remittances
Private Banks	74.2
Public Sector Banks	17.3
Foreign Banks	8.5
Total	**100.0**

Table 2: Country-wise Share in Inward Remittances

Per cent

Source Country	Share in Total Remittances
United Arab Emirates	26.9
United States	22.9
Saudi Arabia	11.6
Qatar	6.5
Kuwait	5.5
Oman	3.0
United Kingdom	3.0
Malaysia	2.3
Canada	1.0
Hong Kong	0.9
Australia	0.7
Germany	0.6
Italy	0.05
Philippines	0.03
Others	14.8
Total	**100.0**

Table 3: State-wise Share in Inward Remittances

Per cent

Destination State	Share in total remittances
Kerala	19.0
Maharashtra	16.7
Karnataka	15.0
Tamil Nadu	8.0
Delhi	5.9
Andhra Pradesh	4.0

Uttar Pradesh	3.1
West Bengal	2.7
Gujarat	2.1
Punjab	1.7
Bihar	1.3
Rajasthan	1.2
Goa	0.8
Haryana	0.8
Madhya Pradesh	0.4
Orissa	0.4
Jharkhand	0.3
Uttaranchal	0.2
Puducherry	0.2
Chandigarh	0.2
Jammu and Kashmir	0.2
Assam	0.1
Himachal Pradesh	0.1
Chhattisgarh	0.1
Others	15.5
Total	100.0

Note: "Others" also includes those remittances for which banks could not identify the specific destination and therefore covered such transactions under "Others".

❏ **India Post Payment Bank (IPPB)**

Launched: The Prime Minister launched the India Post Payments Bank (IPPB) at Talkatora Stadium in New Delhi on 1 September 2018.

Parent organization	:	India Post
Headquarters	:	New Delhi, India

Important Facts: the India Post Payments Bank, banking services will conveniently reach the remotest places in the country, and the people living there. There are over 1.5 lakh post offices and over three lakh postmen or "grameen dak sevaks" who are connected to the people of the country. Now they shall be empowered with smartphones and digital devices to provide financial services.

It will enable money transfer, transfer of government benefits, bill payments and other services such as investment and insurance.

IPPB will also facilitate digital transactions, and help deliver the benefits of schemes such as Pradhan Mantri Fasal Bima Yojana, which provide assistance to farmers.

IPPB shall reach over 1.5 lakh post offices across the country.

❑ **World Economic Outlook Report – 2018**

Released In: In the month of April International Monetary Fund's (IMF) released World Economic Outlook.

The findings of IMF

The prospects for the world economy have improved.

The world economic growth accelerates from 3.1% in 2016 to 3.5% in 2017, and 3.6% in 2018.

Growth in advanced economies is projected to rise from 1.7% in 2016 to 2% in 2017 and 2018.

Emerging markets will grow at 4.5% in 2017, and 4.8% in 2018, compared with growth of 4.1% in 2016.

China will see growth decelerating from 6.7% in 2016 to 6.6% and 6.2% in 2017 and 2018, respectively.

India's growth, in contrast, will accelerate from 6.8% in 2016 to 7.2% and 7.7% over the next two years.

The IMF also warns that high income inequality is likely to persist.

The IMF warns that emerging markets, including India, will find the external conditions for growth less supportive than in the post-2000 period.

Tightening monetary conditions in the advanced world spell lower capital flows.

Largest economies in the world by GDP

1. United States   2. China   3. Japan

4. Germany   5. Britai   6. India

❑ **Sanitary Napkins " SUVIDHA"**

The launch of: 'Suvidha' 100% Oxi-biodegradable Sanitary Napkin, under the "Pradhan Mantri Bhartiya - Janaushadhi Pariyojana (PMBJP)".

Important Fact: The affordable sanitary napkin will be available over 3200 "Janaushadhi Kendras" across India and would ensure 'Swachhta, Swasthya and Suvidha' for the underprivileged Women of India.

This step taken by the Department of Pharmaceuticals will ensure the achievement of Prime Minster Shri Narendra Modi's vision of Affordable and Quality Healthcare for All.

According to the National Family Health Survey 2015-16, about 58 percent of women aged between 15 to 24 years use locally prepared napkins, sanitary napkins and tampons.

Further, about 78 percent women in urban areas use hygienic methods of protection during menstrual period; only 48 percent women in rural areas have access to clean sanitary napkins.

The average price of sanitary napkins available in the market today is around Rs. 8 per pad, whereas now with the launch of the SUVIDHA napkins at Rs. 2.50 per pad, this will go a long way in making the basic hygiene requirement aid for Women affordable for the underprivileged sections.

❑ **Global Findex Report – 2018**

In 2011 the World Bank — with funding from the Bill & Melinda Gates Foundation — launched the Global Findex database, the world's most comprehensive data set on how adults save, borrow, make payments, and manage risk.

Released by : World Bank

Date : 19th April 2018

Focused on : to represent the conditions of financial inclusion

Important facts of the report: The report states that though financial inclusion is on the rise globally, gaps still remain there across the countries. Men still are ahead of women to have an account in a bank. Globally, 69 percent of adults now have an account at a bank or have enrolled themselves on a mobile money provider.

India's situation: According to World Bank, India has 19 crore adults without a bank account despite the success of the ambitious Jan Dhan Yojana, making it the world's second largest unbanked population after that of China. In India, 60 percent of the unbanked adults are women. In India, around 4 in 10 unbanked adults are in the age group of 15 to 24 years.

❑ **Payment Bank**

The Reserve Bank of India (RBI) regulates and supervises Public Sector and Private Sector Banks. Under the Provisions of the Banking Regulation Act, 1949 article 22(1). **Payments Banks and Small Finance Banks** are a New Model of banks conceptualized by the Reserve Bank of India(RBI). **11 Payment Banks and 10 Small Finance Banks have received license from Reserve Bank of India to start banking operations in India**. Small Finance Banks and Payment Banks are new age banks and given the strength of the bank, expertise. The list of RBI approved for provisional Payments Bank licenses are 11 in which 6 active Payment Banks are as following :

1. Aditya Birla Payments Bank

2. Airtel Payments Bank

3. India Post Payments Bank

4. Fino Payments Bank

5. Jio Payments Bank

6. Paytm Payments Bank

❑ **GDP V/S GVA**

GDP	**GVA**
• GDP represent Consumer side or demand side of Indian Economy.	• On the other hand GVA represent producer side or supply side of Indian economy.
• GDP is the method to measure of demand side of economy.	• On the other hand GVA is the method to measure of supply side of economy.
• CSO started calculating economical activities through GDP on 15 January, 2018.	• On the other hand Government of India used GVA as a tool to calculating growth rate of economy.

Note: RBI also adapted the concept of GDP to calculating the growth rate of economy.

- Method of GDP is adapted worldwide.

- Globally, Calculating growth rate of economies by the tool of GDP.

- International organization also used the tool of GDP, calculating the growth rate.

❑ **Moral hazard**

Moral hazard is a situation in which one party gets involved in a risky event knowing that it is protected against the risk and the other party will incur the cost. It arises when both the parties have incomplete information about each other.

Moral hazard is idea that a party protected in some way from risk will act differently than if they didn't have that protection. We encounter moral hazard every day—tenured professors becoming indifferent lecturers, people with theft insurance being less vigilant about where they park, salaried salespeople taking long breaks, and so on.

Moral hazard is usually applied to the insurance industry. Insurance companies worry that by offering payouts to protect against losses from accidents, they may actually encourage risk-taking, which results in them paying more in claims. Insurers fear that a "don't worry, it's insured" attitude leads to policyholders with collision insurance driving recklessly or fire-insured home owners smoking in bed.

In context of Companies Bankruptcy: It is a financial condition where a firm/individual is unable to repay debts to creditors. Under India's Insolvency and Bankruptcy Code 2016, a bankrupt entity is a debtor who has been adjudged as bankrupt by an adjudicating authority through passing a bankruptcy order.

❑ **RBI Report 2017-18 on Demonetisation**

Issued Date : 29 August, 2018

Important facts related to report : According to the report, after verification and reconciliation, the total value of the Rs. 500 and Rs. 1000 notes as on November, 8, 2016 the day before note ban came into effect, was Rs. 15,417.93 lakh Crore. The total value of the such notes returned from circulation was Rs. 15,310.73 Lakh Crore.

According to the RBI data, the value of banknotes in circulation increased by 33.7% over the year to Rs. 18,037 Lakh Crore as at end March 2018.

Over 99% of the Rs. 500 and Rs. 1000 notes that were withdrawn from circulation in November 2016 were returned.

❑ **Current Economy Vocabulary**

(a) Angel Investor

An angel investor is a wealthy individual who provides funding for a startup, often in exchange for an ownership stake in the company. Typically, angels, as they are known, will invest somewhere between $25,000-500,000 to help a company get started. In many cases, angels are the last option for startups that don't qualify for bank financing and may be too small to interest a venture capital (VC) firm. Unlike VCs, however, which demand aggressive revenue growth quickly, angels are more concerned with the commitment and passion of the founders and the larger market opportunity that they have identified. While angels don't want to lose their money, they aren't typically as focused on making a quick buck as VCs are.

(b) Non Performing Assets

A nonperforming asset (NPA) refers to a classification for loans or advances that are in default or are in arrears on scheduled payments of principal or interest. In most cases, debt is classified as nonperforming when loan payments have not been made for a period of 90 days. While 90 days of nonpayment is the standard, the amount of elapsed time may be shorter or longer depending on the terms and conditions of each loan.

Types of Nonperforming Assets

Although the most common nonperforming assets are term loans, there are six other ways loans and advances are NPAs:

- Overdraft and cash credit (OD/CC) accounts left out-of-order for more than 90 days

- Agricultural advances whose interest or principal installment payments remain overdue for two crop/ harvest seasons for short duration crops or overdue one crop season for long duration crops

- Bill overdue for more than 90 days for bills purchased and discounted

- Expected payment is overdue for more than 90 days in respect of other accounts

- Non-submission of stock statements for 3 consecutive quarters in case of cash-credit facility

- No activity in the cash credit, EPC, or PCFC account for more than 91 days

Banks are required to classify nonperforming assets in one of three categories according to how long the asset has been non-performing: sub-standard assets, doubtful assets, and loss assets. A sub-standard asset is an asset classified as an NPA for less than 12 months. A doubtful asset is an asset that has been non-performing for more than 12 months. Loss assets are assets with losses identified by the bank, auditor, or inspector and have not been fully.

(c) Black Money

Black money is money earned through any illegal activity controlled by country regulations. Black money proceeds are usually received in cash from underground economic activity and, as such, are not taxed. Recipients of black money must hide it, spend it only in the or attempt to give it the appearance of legitimacy through money laundering.

(d) Parallel Economy

Parallel economy, based on the black money or unaccounted money, is a big menace to the Indian economy. It is also a cause of big loss in the tax-revenues for the government. As such, it needs to be curbed. Its elimination will benefit the economy in more than one way.

In a general way, we can define black economy as the money that is generated by activities that are kept secret, in the sense that these are not reported to the authorities. As such, this money is also not accounted to (he fiscal authorities i.e., taxes are not paid on this money.

(e) Tax Haven Economy

Tax havens are, on the other hand, the problem continues, by the fact that adversely affect the budgetary revenue of countries with higher taxation and thereby give rise to increased tax avoidance, particularly that law, lawful and unlawful migration to the capital, causing financial instability, and by circumvention of financial control, financial crises.The pressure group Tax Justice Network estimated that losses arising as a result of the global system of taxation through tax havens up to 255 billion. doll ars per year, but these figures are not accepted unanimously.

(f) Shell Company

Theoretically, shell companies are companies without active business operations or significant assets. They can be set up by business people for both legitimate and illegitimate purposes.

Illegitimate purposes for registering a shell company include hiding particulars of ownership from the law enforcement, laundering unaccounted money and avoiding tax. With the shell company as a front, all transactions are shown on paper as legitimate business transactions, thereby turning black money into white. In this process, the business person also avoids paying tax on the laundered money.

India, however, does not have a concrete definition of shell companies. Shell companies are not defined in any law or act. However, US has defined the shell companies under their Securities Act. They have taken up the basic definition, hence making it the commonly used one. The US Securities Act defines shell companies as -

"Securities Act Rule 405 and Exchange Act Rule 12b-2 define a Shell Company as a company, other than an asset-backed issuer, with no or nominal operations; and either:

- No or nominal assets assets consisting of cash and cash equivalents; or

- Assets consisting of any amount of cash and cash equivalents and nominal other assets."

(g) Phishing

Phishing is a cybercrime in which a target or targets are contacted by email, telephone or text message by someone posing as a legitimate institution to lure individuals into providing sensitive data such as personally identifiable information, banking and credit card details, and passwords.The information is then used to access important accounts and can result in identity theft and financial loss.

(h) Identity theft

Identity theft is the unauthorized collection of personal information and its subsequent use for criminal reasons such as to open credit cards and bank accounts, redirect mail, set up cellphone service, rent vehicles and even get a job. These actions can mean severe consequences for the victim, who will be left with bills, charges and a damaged credit score.

There are many ways in which an individual's identity can be stolen, but people may be particularly vulnerable to this crime online, where savvy criminals can gain access to personal information through a number of avenues. According to the U.S. Federal Trade Commission, approximately nine million Americans have their identities stolen each year. This theft is increasingly being perpetrated electronically.

(i) Black Hat Hacker

A black hat hacker is a person who attempts to find computer security vulnerabilities and exploit them for personal financial gain or other malicious reasons. This differs from white hat hackers, which are security specialists employed to use hacking methods to find security flaws that black hat hackers may exploit.

Black hat hackers can inflict major damage on both individual computer users and large organizations by stealing personal financial information, compromising the security of major systems, or shutting down or altering the function of websites and networks.

(j) White Hat Hacker

A white hat hacker is a computer security specialist who breaks into protected systems and networks to test and asses their security. White hat hackers use their skills to improve security by exposing vulnerabilities before malicious hackers (known as black hat hackers) can detect and exploit them. Although the methods used are similar, if not identical, to those employed by malicious hackers, white hat hackers have permission to employ them against the organization that has hired them.

(k) Venture Capital

Venture capital is financing that investors provide to companies and small businesses that are believed to have potential. Venture capital generally comes from well-off investors, investment banks and any other financial institutions. However, it does not always take just a monetary form; it can be provided in the form of technical or managerial expertise.

(l) Foreign Portfolio Investment

Foreign portfolio investment (FPI) consists of securities and other financial assets passively held by foreign investors. It does not provide the investor with direct ownership of financial assets and is relatively liquid depending on the volatility of the market. Foreign portfolio investment differs from foreign direct investment (FDI), in which a domestic company runs a foreign firm, because although FDI allows a company to maintain better control over the firm held abroad, it may face more difficulty selling the firm at a premium price in the future.

(m) Foreign Direct Investment

Foreign direct investment (FDI) is an investment made by a firm or individual in one country into business interests located in another country. Generally, FDI takes place when an investor establishes foreign business operations or acquires foreign business assets, including establishing ownership or controlling interest in a foreign company. Foreign direct investments are distinguished from portfolio investments in which an investor merely purchases equities of foreign-based companies.

(n) Foreign Institutional Investors

A foreign institutional investor (FII) is an investor or investment fund registered in a country outside of the one in which it is investing. Institutional investors most notably include hedge funds, insurance companies, pension funds and mutual funds. The term is used most commonly in India and refers to outside companies investing in the financial markets of India.

(o) State finance Corporations-SFGs

The State Finance Corporations (SFCs) are the integral part of institutional finance structure in the country. SEC promotes small and medium industries of the states. Besides,

SFCs are helpful in ensuring balanced regional development, higher investment, more employment generation and broad ownership of industries.

At present there are 18 state finance corporations (out of which 17 SFCs were established under SFC Act 1951). Tamil Nadu Industrial Investment Corporation Ltd. established under Company Act, 1949, is also working as state finance corporation.

(p) Corporate Social Responsibility

Corporate social responsibility (CSR) is a self-regulating business model that helps a company be socially accountable — to itself, its stakeholders, and the public. By practicing corporate social responsibility, also called corporate citizenship, companies can be conscious of the kind of impact they are having on all aspects of society including economic, social, and environmental. To engage in CSR means that, in the normal course of business, a company is operating in ways that enhance society and the environment, instead of contributing negatively to it.

(q) Mega Food Park

The Scheme of Mega Food Park aims at providing a mechanism to link agricultural production to the market by bringing together farmers, processors and retailers so as to ensure maximizing value addition, minimizing wastage, increasing farmers income and creating employment opportunities particularly in rural sector. The Mega Food Park Schcmc is based on "Cluster" approach and envisages creation of state of art support infrastructure in a well-defined agri / horticultural zone for setting up of modern food processing units in the industrial plots provided in the park with well-established supply chain. Mega food park typically consist of supply chain infrastructure including collection centers, primary processing centers, central processing centers, cold chain and around 30-35 fully developed plots for entrepreneurs to set up food processing units.

(r) Prime Lending Rate

The ultimate objective of Monetary Policy of the Reserve Bank of India (RBI)is to target Growth and Inflation. In a bank-centric economy that India is, playing with the interest rates can prove to be pivotal to control both growth and inflation. Changes in interest rates results in an immediate change in short term money market rates and inter alia, banks' lending and deposit rates. This change ultimately results in a change in the demand and supply of money. Thus, it is of utmost importance that the lending and the deposit rates set by the banks reflect the changes in the Monetary Policy (here interest rates). Failure of such a transmission would render it difficult for the RBI to tackle Growth and Inflation in an economy like India.

(s) Base Rate

Base rate is the minimum rate set by the Reserve Bank of India below which banks are not allowed to lend to its customers. Base rate is decided in order to enhance transparency in the credit market and ensure that banks pass on the lower cost of fund to their customers. Loan pricing will be done by adding base rate and a suitable spread depending on the credit risk premium.

(t) Legal Tender Money

Legal tender is any official medium of payment recognized by law that can be used to extinguish a public or private debt, or meet a financial obligation. The national currency is legal tender in practically every country. A creditor is obligated to accept legal tender toward repayment of a debt. Legal tender can only be issued by the national body that is authorized to do so, such as the U.S. Treasury in the United States and the Royal Canadian Mint in Canada.

(u) Twin Balance Sheet Problem

A **balance sheet** is a statement of an institution's assets and liabilities. ... Even the RBI publishes its **balance sheet**. But, the **'twin balance sheet' issue** refers to the problematic **balance sheets** of Indian companies and banks—meaning, both the lenders and borrowers are under stress.

(v) Capital Adequacy Ratio

The Capital Adequacy Ratio (CAR) is a measure of a bank's available capital expressed as a percentage of a bank's risk-weighted credit exposures. The Capital Adequacy Ratio, also known as capital-to-risk weighted assets ratio (CRAR), is used to protect depositors and promote the stability and efficiency of financial systems around the world. Two types of capital are measured: tier one capital, which can absorb losses without a bank being required to cease trading, and tier two capital, which can absorb losses in the event of a winding-up and so provides a lesser degree of protection to depositors.

(w) Universal Banking

Universal banking is a system in which banks provide a wide variety of financial services, including commercial and investment services. Universal banking is common in some European countries, including Switzerland. In the United States, however, banks are required to separate their commercial and investment banking services. Proponents of universal banking argue that it helps banks better diversify risk. Detractors think dividing up banks' operations is a less risky strategy.

(x) Core Banking

Today Banking as a business has grown tremendously and transformed itself from only a deposits taking and loan providing system to an institution which provides an entire gamut of products and services under a wide umbrella. All such activities commenced by a bank is called Core Banking. As per pure definition Core banking refers to a centralized system established by a bank which allows its customers to conduct their business irrespective of the bank's branch. Thus, it removes the impediments of geo-specific transactions. In fact, CORE is an acronym for "Centralized Online Real-time Exchange", thus the bank's branches can access applications from centralized data centers.

(y) Blue Chip Company

A blue chip is a nationally recognized, well-established, and financially sound company. Blue chips generally sell high-quality, widely accepted products and services. Blue chip companies are known to weather downturns and operate profitably in the face of adverse economic conditions, which helps to contribute to their long record of stable and reliable growth. The name "blue chip" came about from the game of poker in which the blue chips have the highest value.

(z) Round Tripping

The term 'round-tripping' is self-explanatory. It denotes a trip where a person or thing returns to the place from where the journey began. In the context of black money, it leaves the country through various channels such as inflated invoices, payments to shell companies overseas, the hawala route and so on. After cooling its heels overseas for a while, this money returns in a freshly laundered form; thus completing a round-trip. This route is far from simple or straightforward.

Science & Technology

❑ **Progress of Space Technology**

Indian Space Research Organisation achieved the grand launch from PSLV-C43 on November 29, 2018 from the First Launch Pad (FLP) of Satish Dhawan Space Centre SHAR, Sriharikota and successfully launched India's Hyper spectral Imaging Satellite (HysIS) and 30 international co-passenger satellites. **And in** its thirty ninth flight (PSLV-C37), ISRO's Polar Satellite Launch Vehicle successfully launched the 714 kg Cartosat-2 Series Satellite along with 103 co-passenger satellites on February 15, 2017 from Satish Dhawan Space Centre SHAR, Sriharikota. This was the thirty eighth consecutively successful mission of PSLV. The total weight of all the 104 satellites carried on-board PSLV-C37 was 1378 kg. **As previously India was used to call the** Country of snake charmers but now with efforts of ISRO it has reached to Moon and Mars in the space.

Now, India is focusing to sending an Indian astronaut to space - like human crew module and environment control and life support system - have already been developed by the year 2022 ISRO will become capable to this.

	Date	Launched	Launcher's Satellite	Important Facts/Remarks
1.	6-02-2019	Ariene-5	GSAT-31	India's latest communication satellite, GSAT-31 was successfully launched from the Spaceport in French Guiana. With a lift-off mass of 2536 kg, GSAT-31 will augment the Ku-band transponder capacity in Geostationary Orbit. The satellite will provide continuity to operational services on some of the in-orbit satellites. GSAT-31 derives its heritage from ISRO's earlier INSAT/GSAT satellite series. The satellite provides Indian mainland and island coverage.
2.	24-01-2019	PSLV-C44	Microsat-R & Kalamsat-V2	India's Polar Satellite Launch Vehicle (PSLV-C44) successfully injected Microsat-R and Kalamsat-V2 satellites into their designated orbits.The PSLV-C44 lifted from the First Launch Pad at Satish Dhawan Space Centre SHAR, Sriharikota in its 46th flight.About 13 minutes 26 seconds after lift-off, Microsat-R, an imaging satellite was successfully injected into intended orbit of 274 km. Subsequently, the fourth stage (PS4) of the vehicle was moved to a higher circular orbit of 453 km after two restarts of the stage, to establish an orbital platform for carrying out experiments. Kalamsat-V2, a student payload, first to use PS4 as an orbital platform.
3.	19-12-2018	GSLV-F11	GSAT-7A	Indian Space Research Organisation's (ISRO) Geosynchronous Satellite Launch Vehicle (GSLV-F11) successfully launched the communication satellite GSAT-7A from the Satish Dhawan Space Centre (SDSC) in Sriharikota today.The GSLV-F11 lifted off from the Second Launch Pad carrying 2250 kg GSAT-7A and about 19 minutes later, injected GSAT-7A into a Geosynchronous Transfer Orbit (GTO) of 170.8 km x 39127 km

				which is very close to the intended orbit. An ISRO team lead by Chairman Dr K Sivan, Vikram Sarabhai Space Centre (VSSC) S Somanath, U R Rao Satellite Centre (URSC) Director P Kunhikrishnan, Space Applications Centre (SAC) Director D K Das, SDSC Director S Pandian, Liquid Propulsion Systems Centre (LPSC) Dr V Narayanan and ISRO Propulsion Complex (IPRC) Director T Mookiah witnessed the launch.Mission Director Mohan M and Satellite Director Killedar Pankaj Damodar oversaw the launch proceedings. Soon after the separation of the satellite, ISRO's Master Control Facility (MCF) at Hassan in Karnataka took over the command and control of GSAT-7A.The satellite's health parameters are normal.
4.	05-12-2018	Ariane-5	GSAT-11	India's next generation high throughput communication satellite, GSAT-11 was successfully launched from Kourou launch base, French Guiana by Ariane-5 VA-246. Weighing about 5854 kg, GSAT-11 is the heaviest satellite built by ISRO.GSAT-11 is the fore-runner in the series of advanced communication satellites with multi-spot beam antenna coverage over Indian mainland and Islands. GSAT-11 will play a vital role in providing broadband services across the country. It will also provide a platform to demonstrate new generation applications.GSAT-11 was launched into a Geosynchronous Transfer Orbit and subsequently ISRO's Master Control Facility at Hassan taken over the control of GSAT-11 to perform the initial orbit raising maneuvers using the Liquid Apogee Motor of the satellite for placing it in circular Geostationary Orbit.

| 5. | 29-11-2018 | PSLV-C43 | Hyper spectral Imaging Satellite (HysIS) and 30 international co-passenger satellites. | PSLV-C43 lifted off from the First Launch Pad (FLP) of Satish Dhawan Space Centre SHAR, Sriharikota and successfully launched India's Hyper spectral Imaging Satellite (HysIS) and 30 international co-passenger satellites.Polar Satellite Launch Vehicle (PSLV) is a four stage launch vehicle with alternating solid and liquid stages. PSLV-C43 is the Core Alone version of PSLV, without the six strap-ons.HysIS, the primary satellite of PSLV-C43 mission, weighing about 380 kg, is an earth observation satellite configured around ISRO's Mini Satellite-2 (IMS-2) bus. The primary goal of HysIS is to study the earth's surface in the visible, near infrared and shortwave infrared regions of the electromagnetic spectrum.The co-passengers of HysIS include 1 Micro and 29 Nano satellites from 8 different countries. These satellites have been commercially contracted for launch through Antrix Corporation Limited, the commercial arm of ISRO. |
| 6. | 14-11-2018 | GSLV-MK-IIID2 | GSAT-29 | GSAT-29 satellite with a lift-off mass of 3423 kg, is a multi-beam, multiband communication satellite of India, configured around the ISRO's enhanced I-3K bus. This is the heaviest satellite launched from India.GSAT-29 carries Ka/Ku-band high throughput communication transponders which will bridge the digital divide of users including those in Jammu & Kashmir and North Eastern regions of India. It also carries Q/V-band payload, configured for technology demonstration at higher frequency bands and Geo-stationary High Resolution Camera. carried onboard GSAT-29 spacecraft. An optical communication payload, for the first time, will be utilized for data transmission. |

7.	16-9-2018	PSLV-C42	Nova SAR and S1-4 (together weighing nearly 889 kg)	PSLV-C42 Successfully Launches two foreign satellites from "Satish Dhawan Space Centre (SDSC), SHAR Sriharikota". This mission was designed to launch two earth observation satellites, Nova-SAR and S1-4 (together weighing nearly 889 kg) of M/s Surrey Satellite Technologies Limited (SSTL), United Kingdom under commercial arrangement with Antrix Corporation Limited, Department of Space. Both satellites were injected into 583 km Sun Synchronous Orbit. Nova-SAR is S-Band Synthetic Aperture Radar satellite intended for forest mapping, land use & ice cover monitoring, flood & disaster monitoring.S1-4 is a high resolution Optical Earth Observation Satellite, used for surveying resources, environment monitoring, urban management and for the disaster monitoring.
8.	12-4-2018	PSLV-C41	IRNSS-1-I	India's Polar Satellite Launch Vehicle, in its forty-third flight (PSLV-C41) in XL configuration launched IRNSS-1-I Satellite from First Launch Pad (FLP) of SDSC SHAR, Sriharikota. The 'XL' configuration of PSLV is used for the twentieth time. The IRNSS-1I is the eighth satellite to join the NavIC navigation satellite constellation. Note: the following eight IRNSS satellites have been launched.1- IRNSS 1A, 2- IRNSS 1B 3- IRNSS 1C, 4- IRNSS 1D, 5- IRNSS 1E, 6- IRNSS 1F, 7- IRNSS 1G ,8- IRNSS 1I.(In the year 2017 IRNSS 1H satellite launch could not succeed.)
9.	29-03-2018	GSLV-F08	GSAT-6A	GSLV-F08 is the 12th flight of Geosynchronous Satellite Launch Vehicle (GSLV) and Sixth flight with indigenous Cryogenic Stage. The Launch of GSLV-F08 carrying GSAT-6A took place from the Second Launch Pad (SLP) in Satish Dhawan Space Centre SHAR, Sriharikota.

| 10. | 12-01-2018 | PSLV-C40 | Cartosat-2 Series Satellite | India's Polar Satellite Launch Vehicle, in its forty second flight (PSLV-C40), successfully launched the 710 kg Cartosat-2 Series Satellite for earth observation and 30 co-passenger satellites together weighing about 613 kg at lift-off. PSLV-C40 was launched from the First Launch Pad (FLP) of Satish Dhawan Space Centre (SDSC) SHAR, Sriharikota. The co-passenger satellites comprise one Microsatellite and one Nanosatellite from India as well as 3 Microsatellites and 25 Nanosatellites from six countries, namely, Canada, Finland, France, Republic of Korea, UK and USA. The total weight of all the 31 satellites carried onboard PSLV-C40 is about 1323 kg. |

❑ Proposed Space Plan (2019-20)

	Name of the Mission	Year	Launch Vehicle	Important Facts /Remarks
1.	Gaganyan	2022	GSLV-Mark-3	The Indian Space Research Organisation wants to make the ambitious manned mission Gaganyaan "more and more" indigenous by utilising the facilities available in the country. Addressing a press conference after successfully launching ISRO's earth observation satellite HysIS and 30 other co-passengers into their designated orbits the space agency may have to take outside help for some tests. HysIS means Hyper Spectral Imaging Satellite."In order to meet the Prime Minister's (Narendra Modi) vision (of sending humans to space) by 2022, to undertake some testing we may go abroad.The space agency is aiming to undertake the first unmanned programme under the Gaganyaan project by December 2020. If Gaganyaan is successful, India would become the fourth

				nation to achieve the feat.On the future launches planned by ISRO, "For next year it has planned to undertake almost 12-14 missions." After GSAT-11 in December, next GSAT-7A is there. In January a micro-satellite launched then Chandrayaan-II mission have been under the process. Rs. 10,000-crore mission will be a turning point in India's space journey. Isro has developed some critical technologies like re-entry mission capability, crew escape system, crew module configuration, thermal protection system, deceleration and flotation system, sub-systems of life support system required for Mission Gaganyaan.
2.	Chandra-yaan-2	2019	GSLV-F-10	India's second mission to the Moon is a totally indigenous mission comprising of an Orbiter, Lander and Rover. After reaching the 100 km lunar orbit, the Lander housing the Rover will separate from the Orbiter. After a controlled descent, the Lander will soft land on the lunar surface at a specified site and deploy a Rover.The mission will carry a six-wheeled Rover which will move around the landing site in semi-autonomous mode as decided by the ground commands. The instruments on the rover will observe the lunar surface and send back data, which will be useful for analysis of the lunar soil.The Chandrayaan-2 weighing around 3290 kg and would orbit around the moon and perform the objectives of remote sensing the moon. The payloads will collect scientific information on lunar topography, mineralogy, elemental abundance, lunar exosphere and signatures of hydroxyl and water-ice.The Lander Actuator Performance Test (LAPT) is one of the crucial tests required to be demonstrated for a successful

				soft and safe landing of Vikram (Chandrayaan-2 Lander). To carry out this test, an LAPT module which is a scaled down version of Vikram with all the required hardware was realised for testing in Earth environment. The reason for the scaling down is to compensate the effect of Earth's gravity as compared to Moon's gravity and to match the thrust generation of sea level Liquid Engines as compared to flight engines which will operate in vacuum environment. The module was tethered to a crane hook for conducting the test. To carry out this test, a special test facility was erected at ISRO Propulsion Complex, Mahendragiri.The objective of the test was to assess the closed loop integrated performance of Sensors, Actuators and Navigation, Guidance & Control (NGC) and guidance algorithms below 100 m height. Three tests have been conceived as part of LAPT Phase-2 activities to demonstrate these objectives. First test was conducted to demonstrate Vertical Descent while second Test was conducted to demonstrate Hovering.The third and final test was successfully conducted to demonstrate re-targeting in a Parabolic Trajectory, on 25th Oct 2018 at ISRO Propulsion Complex, Mahendragiri. This test demonstrated the capability of the NGC system of Vikram to meet the mission requirement of safe, soft and precise landing on the lunar surface by steering the module horizontally as well as vertically down to a pre-defined target. With this, all the tests have been completed successfully. This is a major milestone accomplished in Chandrayaan-2 Lander.

| 3. | Aditya - L1 | 2019 | GSLV-
Mark-3 | The Aditya-1 mission was conceived as a 400kg class satellite carrying one payload, the Visible Emission Line Coronagraph (VELC) and was planned to launch in a 800 km low earth orbit. A Satellite placed in the halo orbit around the Lagrangian point 1 (L1) of the Sun-Earth system has the major advantage of continuously viewing the Sun without any occultation/ eclipses. Therefore, the Aditya-1 mission has now been revised to "Aditya-L1 mission" and will be inserted in a halo orbit around the L1, which is 1.5 million km from the Earth. The satellite carries additional six payloads with enhanced science scope and objectives.Aditya-L1 with additional experiments can now provide observations of Sun's Photosphere (soft and hard X-ray), Chromosphere (UV) and corona (Visible and NIR). In addition, particle payloads will study the particle flux emanating from the Sun and reaching the L1 orbit, and the magnetometer payload will measure the variation in magnetic field strength at the halo orbit around L1. These payloads have to be placed outside the interference from the Earth's magnetic field and could not have been useful in the low earth orbit. |

❑ Artificial Intelligence

Artificial intelligence (AI) is the area of computer science focusing on creating machines that can engage on behaviors that humans consider intelligent. John McCarthy, who coined the term in 1956 at the Massachusetts Institute of Technology, defines it as "the science and engineering of making intelligent machines." It is a combination of computer science, physiology, and philosophy.

Artificial Intelligence Includes :

Games playing : programming computers to play games such as chess and checkers

Expert systems : programming computers to make decisions in real-life situations (for example, some expert systems help doctors diagnose diseases based on symptoms)

Natural language : programming computers to understand natural human languages

Neural networks: Systems that simulate intelligence by attempting to reproduce the types of physical connections that occur in animal brains.

Robotics: programming computers to see and hear and react to other sensory stimuli.

Currently, no computer exhibits full artificial intelligence (that is, are able to simulate human behavior).

AI Research : There are two main lines of research :

- Biological, based on the idea that since humans are intelligent. AI should study humans and imitate their psychology or physiology.

- Phenomenal, based on studying and formalizing common sense facts about the world and the problems that the world presents to the achievement of goals.

- The two approaches interact to some extent.

Advantages of Artificial Intelligence :

- Machines can be used to take on complex and stressful work that would be otherwise performed by humans.

- Machines can complete the task faster than a human assigned to do the same task. Use of robotics to discover unexplored landscape, outer space and also be useful in our home activities.

- Less danger, injury and stress to humans as the work is done by a artificially intelligent machine.Aiding of mental, visually and hearing impaired individuals

- Used for games to create an atmosphere where you don't feel like you are playing against just a machine.

Disadvantages of Artificial Intelligence:

It lacks the human touch. Its human qualities are sometimes ignored. It has ability to replace a human job. It gives rise to humans feeling insecure and may have the fear of losing their job. Human capabilities can be replaced using a machine and therefore can foster feelings of inferiority among workers and staff. Artificial Intelligence can malfunction and do the opposite of what they are programmed to do. It has may corrupt the younger generation. There is no filtering of information. The type of technology can be misused to cause mass scale destruction.

Artificial Intelligence and World: The development in the field of Artificial Intelligence have been started from 2010 at the rate of 60% in which top five countries are as following;

America: Companies like IBM, Microsoft, Google, Facebook and Amazon have invested more than 10 billion dollars on Artificial Intelligence which has grown this market in America and made it top most country in this field.

Britain: Deepmind technology has been established to promote the Artificial Intelligence in the country.

Japan: The country has published more than 11 thousands Research Paper on Artificial Intelligence.

Germany: The country is making efforts to become the Hub of Artificial Intelligence.

China: Planning to become a Centre of highest level innovation in Artificial Intelligence by the year of 2030.

Note: India is making hardcore effort to become top country in the Field of Articical Intelligence in upcoming 20 years.

❑ **Super Computers in India**

Pratyush (World record 45th rank) : The latest supercomputer at IITM,Pune "Pratyush" is a Cray-XC40 LC [Liquid Cooled] System with 3315 nodes running Intel Xeon Broadwell E5-2695 processors with a peak performance of 4,006 TFLOPS and a total system memory of 414TB. The system is composed of 18 Compute cabinets and uses Cray's Aries NOC with Dragonfly Interconnect network topology. In addition, the system consists of 16 Intel KNL 7210 accelerator nodes with a peak performance of 42.56TFLOPS and a total memory of 1.5TB.

The entire system operates on Cray's customized Linux OS, called Cray Linux Environment. The cluster supports architecture specific compilers from Cray as well as Intel and open-source GNU compilers. System also hosts architecture specific parallel libraries like OPENMP, MPI, libsci, Intel Cluster software etc. Applications like GFS, WRF,ROMS,CFS are available on the system for weather forecasting. To facilitate users with parallel program development, DDT parallel debugger and profiler is enabled on the system. The system uses PBS Pro as Workload Manager.

Mihr (World record 73rd rank): Mihir is the fastest supercomputer in India with a maximum speed of 6.8 petaflops at a total cost of INR 438.9 Crore working at National Center for Medium Range Weather Forecast (NCMRWF) Noida.

SRECC (World Record 488th rank): Functioning at Indian Institute of Science

PARAM Yuva II: Unveiled on 8 February 2013, this supercomputer was made by Centre for Development of Advanced Computing in a period of three month. It performs at a peak of 524 TFLOPS, about 10 times faster than the present facility, and will consume 35% less energy as compared to the existing facility. Param Yuva II used for research in space, bioinformatics, weather forecasting, seismic data analysis, aeronautical engineering, scientific data processing and pharmaceutical development. Educational institutes like the Indian Institutes of Technology and National Institutes of Technology can be linked to the computer through the national knowledge network. This computer is a stepping stone towards building the future petaflop-range supercomputers in India.

SAGA: SAGA built by ISRO, is capable of performing at 450,000 gigaflop/s (450 teraflop/s). It uses about 400 NVIDIA Tesla C2070 GPUs and 300 NVIDIA Tesla M2090 GPUs for acceleration and 400 Intel Intel QuadCore Xeon CPUs and 330 Intel Intel HexCore Xeon CPUs for proceesing. Storage Capacity is 120 TeraBytes.

EKA: EKA is a supercomputer built by the Computational Research Laboratories with hardware provided by Hewlett-Packard. This is developed by Tata sons. It is capable of performing at 132800 gigaflop/s or 132 teraflop/s.

VIRGO: Indian Institute of Technology, Madras has a 91.1 teraflop/s machine called Virgo. It is ranked as 364 in the Top 500 November-2012 list. It has 292 computer nodes, 2 master nodes, 4 storage nodes and has tota l computing power 97 TFlops.

Vikram-100: Inaugurated on 26 June 2015, by Prof. U. R. Rao at the Physical Research Laboratory, the Vikram-100 is a High Performance Computing (HPC) Cluster (named after eminent scientist Dr Vikram Sarabhai) with more than 100 teraflops of sustained performance. Currently, the Vikram-100 HPC is 13th fastest supercomputer in India.

Cray XC40: SERC IISc has procured the super computer XC40 from Cray Inc. It was up for trials up to 25 January 2015.

6

Programmes, Policies, Apps & Portals

Central Policies and Programmes

S. N.	Policy/Programmes Name	Initiative	Department/Ministry	Important Facts/Features
1.	Swajal Programme	20-02-2018	Ministry of Drinking Water & Sanitation	The Union Minister of Drinking Water and Sanitation. Inaugurated new Swajal Project at Bagori with a budget of more than 32 lakh rupees. Swajal is a community owned drinking water programme for sustained drinking water supply.
2.	Bharat QR Codes	21-02-2018	Launched by Union Government	Bharat QR is P2M (Person to Merchant) Mobile payment solution. This solution is mutually derived among NPCI, Visa and MasterCard payment networks. Once the BQR codes are deployed on Merchant locations, user can pay the utility bills using BQR enabled mobile banking apps without sharing any user credentials to the merchant. It is a quick method of payment.
3.	"NITI Forum for Northeast"	21-02-2018	Ministry for Development of North-East Region	The NITI Forum for Northeast tasked to identify various constraints on the way of accelerated, inclusive and sustainable economic growth in the North East Region of the country and to recommend suitable interventions for addressing identified constraints.

				The Forum may examine and address any other issues which are of importance but not specifically spelled out in its Terms of Reference. It may devise its own procedure to conduct its business/meetings/fields visits or constitution of Sub-Groups etc.
				The forum was co-chaired by the Vice-Chairman of NITI Aayog and Minister of State (I/C), Ministry of Development of Northeastern Region (DoNER).
4.	National Nutrition Mission,	08-03-2018	Ministry of Women and Child Development	The Prime Minister launched the program "National Nutrition Mission" at Jhunjhunu District, Rajasthan. The National Nutrition Mission (NNM) has been set up with a three year budget of Rs.9046.17 crore commencing from 2017-18.
				The NNM is a comprehensive approach towards raising nutrition level in the country on a war footing. It will comprise mapping of various Schemes contributing towards addressing malnutrition, including a very robust convergence mechanism, ICT based Real Time Monitoring system, incentivizing States/UTs for meeting the targets, incentivizing Anganwadi Workers (AWWs) for using IT based tools, eliminating registers used by AWWs, introducing measurement of height of children at the Anganwadi Centres (AWCs), Social Audits, setting-up Nutrition Resource Centres, involving masses through Jan Andolan for their participation on nutrition through various activities, among others.
				NM targets to reduce stunting, under-nutrition, anemia (among young children, women and adolescent girls) and reduce low birth weight by 2%, 2%, 3% and 2% per annum respectively.

5.	Integrated Scheme for Development of Silk Industry	21-03-2018	Ministry of Textiles	The Cabinet Committee on Economic Affairs given its approval for Central Sector Scheme "Integrated Scheme for Development of Silk Industry" for the next three years from 2017-18 to 2019-20 a total allocation of Rs.2161.68 Crore has been approved for the implementation. The core objective of the scheme is to improve the productivity and quality of silk through R&D intervention. The focus of R&D intervention is to promote improved cross¬breed silk and the import substitute Bivoltine silk so that Bivotine silk production in India enhances to such a level that raw silk imports become nil by 2022.
6.	'Samagra Siksha'	24-05-2018	Ministry of Human Resource Development	An integrated Scheme for school education extending support to States from pre-school to senior secondary levels. The Scheme is a paradigm shift in the conceptual design of school education by treating 'school' holistically as a continuum from pre-school, primary, upper primary, secondary and senior secondary levels.
7.	Seva Bhoj Yojana	01-012018	Ministry of Culture	Government of India has introduced a new scheme namely 'Seva Bhoj Yojana' with a total outlay of Rs. 325.00 Crores for Financial Years 2018-19 and 2019-20. The objective of the scheme is to lessen the financial burden of Charitable Religious Institutions who provide Food/Prasad/Langar (Community Kitchen)/Bhandara free of cost without any discrimination to Public/Devotees.
8.	Shaadi Shagun Yojana	9-08-2018	Ministry of Minorities	The scheme was launched by Prime Minster of India with the aim to empower women comes under the minorities group especially Muslims.

				The scheme also promotes the girls education in minority communities who are willing to continue their higher education. Under this scheme selected member will be given the sum of Rs. 51000 at the time of their wedding and with this amount they can continue their Bachelors Degree.
9.	Pravasi Kaushal Vikas Yojna	4-01-2017	by the Ministry of External Affairs	PKVY is a skill development initiative for which MEA and the Ministry of Skill Development and Entrepreneurship (MSDE) had signed a Memorandum of Understanding (MoU) for its implementation. The main objective of the scheme is to provide training and certification to entire Indian workforce who keen on overseas employment in select sectors and job roles, in line with international standards, to facilitate overseas employment opportunities.
10.	Pradhan Mantri Gramin Digital Saksharta Abhiyan	8-02-2017	Cabinet approval for PMGDISHA	The Union Cabinet has approved 'Pradhan Mantri Gramin Digital Saksharta Abhiyan' (PMGDISHA) to make 6 crore rural households digitally literate. PMGDISHA is expected to be one of the largest digital literacy programmes in the world.
11.	'Rashtriya Vayoshri Yojana'	1-04-2017	Launched by the Ministry of Social Justice &- Empowerment	The scheme was launched with the objective to provide Physical Aids and As sisted-living Devices for Senior citizens be longing to BPL category'. It will be implemented by an agency of, 'Artificial Limbs Manufacturing Corporation (ALIMCO)', (a PSU under M/o SJ&E), which will undertake one-year free maintenance of the aids & assisted living devices. The scheme aims to strengthen the Senior Citizens to overcome their age-related physical impairment and to lead a dignified and productive life with minimal dependence on caregivers or other members of the family.

12.	SATH program	10-06-2017	'Sustainable Action for Transforming Human Capital'	The vision of the program is to initiate trans formation in the education and health sectors. SATH aims to identify and build three future 'role model' states for health systems and to develop a roadmap of intervention and program governance structure and also to set up monitoring and tracking mechanisms, hand-hold state institutions through the execution stage and provide support on a range of institutional measures to achieve the end objectives. The programme will be executed by NITI along with McKinsey & Company and IPE Global consortium.
13.	National Mission on Cultural Mapping of India'	18-06-2017	By Ministry of Culture	The Ministry of Culture launched the National Mission on Cultural Mapping of India' in the year of commemoration of the birth centenary of Pandit Deen Dayal Upadhyay, who was born at Mathura. The mission is a part of the 'Ek Bharat Shreshtha Bharat' umbrella. It was launched with a vision that no cultural talent or heritage should remain unattended; heritage should be nurtured, conserved and used as an icon to learn from the past, and also to propagate our cultural talent across all boundaries. The scheme is set to cover all the Blocks of the country, involving a total of 6.40 Lakh villages over the span of next 3 years.
14.	National Biopharma Mission	30-06-2017	Ministry of Science & Technology	The first ever Industry-Academia mission to accelerate biopharmaceutical development in India. The aim of the Mission is to "Enable and nurture an ecosystem for preparing India's technological and product development capabilities in biopharmaceuticals to a level that will be globally competitive over the next decade, and transform the health standards of India's population through affordable product development"

				It is a flagship program of the Government of India in collaboration with World Bank. The total amount for investment is USD 250 million with USD 125 million as a loan from world Bank.
15.	Pradhan Mantri Vaya Vandana Yojana (PMVVY)	21-07-2017	Officially Launched by Mr.Arun Jaitely	PMVVY is a Pension Scheme announced by the Government of India exclusively for the senior citizens aged 60 years and above. Scheme provides an assured return of 8% p.a. payable monthly (equivalent to 8.30% p.a effective) for 10 years.
16.	Swasth Bachche, Swasth Bharat' Programme	21-08-2017	Ministry of Human Resource Development	Swasth Bachche, Swasth Bharat' Programme, an initiative of Kendriya Vidyalaya Sangathan to prepare a physical Health and Fitness Pro file Card of Kendriya Vidyalaya students, it was launched in Kochi. Swasth Bachche, Swasth Bharat programme aims to provide a comprehensive and inclusive report card for children covering all age groups and children of different abilities. Swasth Bachche, Swasth Bharat programme intends to imbibe values of Olympics and Paralympics amongst students.
17.	Mentor India	23-08-2017	NITI Aayog	NITI Aayog's Atal Innovation Mission (AIM), Mentor India is a flagship program of Government of India to promote innovation and entrepreneurship which aims to engage leaders who can dedicate 1 – 2 hours every week in one or more labs and enable school students to experience, learn and practice future skills such as design and computational thinking. Mentor India is as a strategic nation-building initiative to engage leaders who can guide and mentor schools students in 900+ Atal Tinkering Labs (ATL) established by AIM in schools across India.

18.	Pradhan Mantri Matru Vandana Yojana	01-092017	Ministry of Women & Child Development	PMMVY is implemented by the Ministry of Women & Child Development in collaboration with State Governments. The objectives of the scheme are: (i) providing partial compensation for the wage loss in terms of cash incentives so that the woman can take adequate rest before and after delivery of the first living child, (ii) the cash incentives provided would lead to improved health seeking behaviour amongst the Pregnant Women and Lactating Mothers (PW&LM).
19.	Pradhan Mantri Sahaj Bijli Har Ghar Yojana – "Saubhagya"	25-09-2017	Ministry of Power	A new scheme "Pradhan Mantri Sahaj Bijli Har Ghar Yojana – "Saubhagya" is to ensure electrification of all willing households in the country in rural as well as urban areas. The Government of India will provide largely funds for the Scheme to all States/UTs.
20.	Intensified Mission Indradhanush	08-10-2017	Prime Minister Shri Narendra Modi initiated the program from his hometown Vadnagar, Gujrat	The Prime Minister launched the Intensified Mission Indradhanush, to accelerate progress towards the goal of full immunization cover age. It will provide greater focus on urban areas and other pockets of low immunization coverage.
21.	Sampoorna Bima Gram (SBG) Yojana	13-10-2017	Ministry of Communications	The Sampoorna Bima Gram (SBG) Yojana and Postal Life Insurance schemes were launched to provide banking services and affordable life insurance services to people living in rural areas of the country through the postal network. The primary objective of this scheme is to identify at least one village (having a minimum of 100 households) in each of the revenue districts of the country, wherein endeavour will be made to cover all households of that identified village with a minimum of one RPLI (Rural Postal Life Insurance) policy.

22.	RO-RO Ferry Service (Roll on- Roll off)	22-10-2017	PM Inaugurated in Gujrat	The term ro-ro is generally reserved for large ocean-going vessels which have either built-in or shore-based ramps that allow the cargo to be efficiently rolled on and off the vessel when in port. This is in opposite to the lift-on and lift-off (lo-lo) vessels, which use a crane to load and unload cargo. Ro-Ro service is a first of its kind in India; the ferry will be able to carry up to 100 vehicles (cars, buses and trucks) and 250 passengers between the two ports.
23.	'Adopt a Heritage Scheme'	27-10-2017	Ministry of Tourism	The 'Adopt a Heritage Scheme' of Ministry of Tourism was launched on World Tourism Day i.e. 27th September, 2017 by the President of India. This scheme is a unique endeavour of Ministry of Tourism in close collaboration with Ministry of Culture and Archaeological Survey of India (ASI) which envisages developing monuments, heritage and tourist sites across India and making them tourist friendly to enhance their tourism potential and cultural importance, in a planned and phased manner.
24.	Deen Dayal SPARSH Yojana (Scholarship for Promootion Of Aptitude & Research)	03-11-2017	Ministry of Communications	A Pan India scholarship program for school children called Deen Dayal SPARSH Yojana to increase the reach of Philately. Under the scheme of SPARSH (Scholarship for Promotion of Aptitude & Research in Stamps as a Hobby), it is proposed to award annual scholarships to children of Standard VI to IX having good academic record and also pursuing Philately as a hobby through a competitive selection process in all postal circle, it is proposed to award 920 scholarships to selected students.

25.	DARPAN – "Digital Advancement of Rural Post Office for A New India"	21-11-2017	Ministry of Communic-ations	The project's objective is to improve the qual ity of service, add value to services and achieve "financial inclusion" of un-banked rural population. The goal of the IT modernization project with an outlay of Rs. 1400 Crore is to provide solution to each Branch Postmaster (BPM) which will enable each of approximately 1.29 Lakhs Branch Post Offices (BOs) to improve the level of services being offered to rural customers across all the states.
26.	National Hydrology Project (NHP)	6-04-2016	Ministry of Water Resources, River Development and Ganga Rejuvenation (MoWR, RD & GR).	The National Hydrology Project (NHP) is in tended for setting up of a system for timely and reliable water resources data acquisition, storage, collation and management. NHP seeks to build capacity of the State and Central sector organisati-ons in water resources management through the use of Information Systems and adoption of State-of-the-art technologies like Remote Sensing. The NHP will help in gathering Hydro-meteorological data which will be stored and accessed by any user at the State/District/village level.
27.	Pradhan Mantri Ujjwala Yojana (PMUY)	1-05-2016	Scheme for Providing Free LPG connections to Women from BPL Households approved by Cabinet Committee on Economic Affairs	It is the first time in the history of the country that the Ministry of Petroleum and Natural Gas would implement a welfare scheme ben efitting crores of women belonging to the poorest households. Pradhan Mantri Ujjwala Yojana-Scheme for Providing Free LPG connections to Women from BPL Households. The Scheme provides a financial support of Rs 1600 for each LPG connection to the BPL households.

| 28. | Shala Asmita Yojana (SAY), | 25-05-2016 | Ministry of Human Resource Development | The aim of this scheme is to keep a record of all information related to each student such as attendance, enrollment, mid-day meal service, learning outcomes and infrastructural facilities, among other things.

The scheme is basically a tracking system for over 25 Crore students from class 1st to 12th.

About 65% of the students between the ages of 5 to 18 years have Aadhar numbers, according to estimates. The students without Aadhar numbers will be provided unique identity number for tracking.

The tracking system is also expected to track leakage and corruption in mid-day meals. |
| 29. | 'Vidyanjali' | 16-06-2016 | A School Volunteer Programme By Ministry Of Human Resource Development | Vidyanjali is a step forward in creating an eco system, wherein education will be attached with imbibing knowledge and improving learning output with a sense of participation and willingness within the people to contribute towards nation building.

The programme is designed to involve volunteers from different walks of life to strengthen the co-scholastic activities in government schools. |

Important Policies Announced by Government of India in the Budget 2018-19

S.N.	Name of the Policies	Salient Features
1.	"Operation Green	A new initiative titled "Operation Green" has been taken for the farmers so that they can get right price and products. For this purpose, a provision of Rs. 500 crore has been made. The government has declared to set a minimum support price of all kharif crops at 1.5 times the cost of production the would increase the farmers' income. For consumers, tax incentives will be given under Operation Greens. The government is focused to make this program on the lines of 'Operation Flood'. 'Operation Greens' shall promote Farmer Producers Organizations (FPOs), agri- logistics, processing facilities, and professional management.

2.	Ayushman Bharat	A flagship programme under Ayushman Bharat is a National Health Protection Scheme, which will cover over 10 crore poor and vulnerable families (approximately 50 crore beneficiaries) providing coverage upto 5 lakh rupees per family per year for secondary and tertiary care hospitalization. This will be the world's largest government funded healthcare programme. Adequate funds will be provided for smooth implementation of this programme.
3.	National Bamboo Mission	The Mission would ensure holistic development of the bamboo sector by addressing complete value chain and establishing effective linkage of producers (farmers) with industry.
		The scheme will benefit directly and indirectly the farmers as well as local artisans and associated personnel engaged in bamboo sector including associated industries.
		States/ districts covered: The Mission will focus on development of bamboo in limited States where it has social, commercial and economical advantage, particularly in the North Eastern region and States including Madhya Pradesh, Maharashtra, Chhattisgarh, Odisha, Karnataka, Uttarakhand, Bihar, Jharkhand, Andhra Pradesh, Telangana, Gujarat, Tamil Nadu and Kerala.

Apps and Portals

Name	Salient Features
BHIM App	BHIM is a biometric payment system app using Aadhar platform, and is based on Unified Payment Interface (UPI) to facilitate e-payments directly through bank. It was launched to stress on the importance of technology and digital transactions. It can be used on all mobile devices, be it a smart phone or a feature phone with or without internet connection, he added.
SAKHI App	The portal is a network for nurturing entrepreneurship and creating business models for low cost products and services in order to empower women and make them self-reliant and self-sufficient.
	The portal provides assistance through its platform for entrepreneurship learning tools, incubation facility, training programs for fund raising, providing mentors, and one-on-one investor meet, provide market survey facility and technical assistance.

SUKAHD YATRA APP	Union Minister for Road Transport & Highways, Shipping, Water Resources, River Development and Ganga Rejuvenation launched a mobile App and Toll-free Emergency number for Highway users. Sukhad Yatra mobile application has been prepared by National Highways Authority of India, NHAI, to empower the Highway user. The key feature of the app includes provision for the user to enter road quality-related information or to report any accident or pothole on the highway. It also provides users with real-time data related to waiting time expected at Plazas and various facilities like points of interest, highway nest/nest mini, etc., available across the highway. A toll-free number, 1033 enable users to report an emergency condition, or highway-related feedback, ambulance/tow away services along the road to ensure rapid response time in emergency across the highway. The service is supported by a multi-lingual support and user location tracking features.
PENCIL WEB PORTAL	The PENCIL is an electronic platform that aims at involving Centre, State, and District, Governments, civil society and the general public in achieving the target of child labour free society. The Standing Operating Procedures (SOPs) was also introduced for the enforcement of a legal framework against child labour. The SOP is aimed at creating a ready reckoner for trainers, practitioners and monitoring agencies to ensure complete prohibition of child labour and protection of adolescents from hazardous labour ultimately leading to Child Labour Free India.
Umang App of EPFO	Retirement fund body Employees Provident Fund Organisation (EPFO) launched View Pension Passbook Service for pensioners on the UMANG App. The UMANG (Unified Mobile Application for New-age Governance) App aims to build common, Unified platform and mobile app. It was launched part of EPFO's plan to go paperless and provide all services online. It will allow pensioners view their pension passbook on mobile phones with the help of Umang app.
Ten New Swachh Iconic Places Launched	Ten new iconic sites have been taken up under phase III of the flagship project Swachh Iconic Places (SIP) of the Swachh Bharat Mission. The places are Raghavendra Swamy Temple (Kurnool, Andhra Pradesh), Hazardwari Palace (Murshidabad, West Bengal) Brahma Sarovar Temple (Kurukshetra, Haryana), Vidurkuti (Bijnor, Uttar Pradesh), Mana village (Chamoli, Uttarakhand), pangong Lake (Leh-Ladakh, J & K), Nagvasuki Temple (Allahabad, Uttar Pradesh), Sabarimala Temple (Kerala) and Kanvashram (Uttarakhand).

National Policies

(i) National Health Policy, 2017

- Assurance Based Approach- Policy advocates progressively incremental Assurance based Approach with focus on preventive and promotive healthcare

- Health Card linked to health facilities- Policy recommends linking the health card to primary care facility for a defined package of services anywhere in the country.

- Patient Centric Approach- Policy recommends the setting up of a separate, empowered medical tribunal for speedy resolution to address disputes /complaints regarding standards of care, prices of services, negligence and unfair practices. Standard Regulatory framework for laboratories and imaging centers, specialized emerging services, etc

- Micronutrient Deficiency- Focus on reducing micronutrient malnourishment and systematic approach to address heterogeneity in micronutrient adequacy across regions.

- Quality of Care- Public hospitals and facilities would undergo periodic measurements and certification of level of quality. Focus on Standard Regulatory Framework to eliminate risks of inappropriate care by maintaining adequate standards of diagnosis and treatment.

- Make in India Initiative- Policy advocates the need to incentivize local manufacturing to provide customized indigenous products for Indian population in the long run.

- Application of Digital Health- Policy advocates extensive deployment of digital tools for improving the efficiency and outcome of the healthcare system and aims at an integrated health information system which serves the needs of all stake-holders and improves efficiency, transparency, and citizen experience.

- Private Sector engagement for strategic purchase for critical gap filling and for achievement of health goals.

(ii) National Steel Policy, 2017

- The new Steel Policy enshrines the long term vision of the Government to give impetus to the steel sector. It seeks to enhance domestic steel consumption and ensure high quality steel production and create a technologically advanced and globally competitive steel industry.

- Create self-sufficiency in steel production by providing policy support & guidance to private manufacturers, MSME steel producers, CPSEs

- Encourage adequate capacity additions,

- Development of globally competitive steel manufacturing capabilities,

- Cost-efficient production

- Domestic availability of iron ore, coking coal & natural gas,

- Facilitating foreign investment

- Asset acquisitions of raw materials &

- Enhancing the domestic steel demand.

- The policy projects crude steel capacity of 300 million tonnes (MT), production of 255 MT and a robust finished steel per capita consumption of 158 Kgs by 2030 - 31, as against the current consumption of 61 Kgs.

- The policy also envisages to domestically meet the entire demand of high grade automotive steel, electrical steel, special steels and alloys for strategic applications and increase domestic availability of washed coking coal so as to reduce import dependence on coking coal from about 85% to around 65% by 2030-31.

(iii) New Metro Rail Policy, 2017

- "Private participation either for complete provision of metro rail or for some unbundled components (like

Automatic Fare Collection, Operation & Maintenance of services etc) will form an essential requirement for all metro rail projects seeking central financial assistance" says the policy, to capitalize on private resources, expertise and entrepreneurship.

- In view of inadequate availability and even absence of last mile connectivity at present, the new policy seeks to ensure it focusing on a catchment area of five kms. on either side of metro stations requiring States to commit in project reports to provide necessary last mile connectivity through feeder services, Non-Motorised Transport infrastructure like walking and cycling pathways and introduction of para-transport facilities. States, proposing new metro projects will be required to indicate in project report the proposals and investments that would be made for such services.

- Seeking to ensure that least cost mass transit mode is selected for public transport, the new policy mandates Alternate Analysis, requiring evaluation of other modes of mass transit like BRTS (Bus Rapid Transit System), Light Rail Transit, Tramways, Metro Rail and Regional Rail in terms of demand, capacity, cost and ease of implementation. Setting up of Urban Metropolitan Transport Authority (UMTA) has been made mandatory which is to prepare Comprehensive Mobility Plans for cities for ensuring complete multi-modal integration for optimal utilization of capacities.

- The new Metro Rail Policy provides for rigorous assessment of new metro proposals and proposes an independent third party assessment by agencies to be identified by the Government like the Institute of Urban Transport and other such Centres of Excellence whose capacities would be augmented, as required in this regard.

(iv) National Women Policy, 2017

- The Ministry of Women and Child Development has prepared the draft National Policy for Women, 2017 after considering suggestions/comments received from stakeholders. The draft has been examined and approved by the Group of Ministers and has been submitted to the Cabinet for consideration.

- The Draft envisions a society in which women attain their full potential and are able to participate as equal partners in all spheres of life.

- The draft policy addresses the diverse needs of women through identified priority areas: (i)Health including food security and nutrition, (ii)Education, (iii) Economy (including agriculture, industry, labour, employment, NRI women, soft power, service sector, science and technology), Violence against women, (iv) Governance and decision making (v) Violence Against Women (vi) Enabling environment (including housing, shelter and infrastructure, drinking water and sanitation, media and culture, sports and social security) (vii) Environment and climate change.

- Draft policy envisages efforts to be taken up to address the special needs of single women such as widows, separated, divorced, never-married and deserted women including women-headed households and single women living within households.

(v) National Intellectual Policy, 2017

- The National IPR Policy is a vision document that aims to create and exploit synergies between all forms of intellectual property (IP), concerned statutes and agencies. It sets in place an institutional mechanism for implementation, monitoring and review. It aims to incorporate and adapt global best practices to the Indian scenario.

- This policy shall weave in the strengths of the Government, research and development organizations, educational institutions, corporate entities including MSMEs, start-ups and other stakeholders in the creation of an innovation-conducive environment, which stimulates creativity and innovation across sectors, as also facilitates a stable, transparent and service-oriented IPR administration in the country.

- The Policy recognizes that India has a well-established TRIPS-compliant legislative, administrative and judicial framework to safeguard IPRs, which meets its international obligations while utilizing the flexibilities provided in the international regime to address its developmental concerns. It reiterates India's commitment to the Doha Development Agenda and the TRIPS agreement.

The Policy lays down the following seven objectives:

i.   IPR Awareness: Outreach and Promotion - To create public awareness about the economic, social and cultural benefits of IPRs among all sections of society.

ii. Generation of IPRs - To stimulate the generation of IPRs.

iii. Legal and Legislative Framework - To have strong and effective IPR laws, which balance the interests of rights owners with larger public interest.

iv. Administration and Management - To modernize and strengthen servicc-oriented IPR administration.

v.   Commercialization of IPRs - Get value for IPRs through commercialization.

vi. Enforcement and Adjudication - To strengthen the enforcement and adjudicatory mechanisms for combating IPR infringements.

vii. Human Capital Development - To strengthen and expand human resources, institutions and capacities for teaching, training, research and skill building in IPRs.

Reports & Index 2018-19

S.N.	Report/ Indexes	Issuing Organization	Countries/ Economies	Top Position	Lowest Position	India's Rank	India's Neighbour's Rank
1	WEF Energy Transition Index 2018	World Economic Forum 15th March 2018	114	1. Sweden 2. Norway 3. Switzerland	114. Zimbabwe 113. S. Africa 112. Kyrgyzstan	78	76. China 86. Pakistan 90. Bangladesh
2	World Happiness Report 2018	U.N. Sustainable Development Solutions Network 14th March 2018	156	1. Finland 2. Norway 3. Denmark	156. Burundi 155. Central African Republic 154. S. Sudan	133 (122 in 2017)	75. Pakistan 101. Bangladesh 116. Sri Lanka
3	International Intellectual Property Index 2018	Global Intellectual Property Centre 8th Feb. 2018	50	1. U.S.A. 2. Britain 3. Sweden	167. Vendzuela 166 Algeria 165. Egypt	44 (43 in 2017)	25. China 29. Russia
4	Democracy Index 2017	Economist Intelligence Unit 31st Jan. 2018	167	1. Norway 2. Iceland 3. Sweden	167. N. Korea 166 Syria 165. Democratic Republic of Congo	42	139. China 110. Pakistan 92. Bangladesh
5	Environmental Performance Index 2018	World Economic Forum 23rd Jan. 2018	180	1. Switzerland 2. France 3. Denmark	180. Burundi 179. Bangladesh 178. Congo	177 (141 in 2016)	70. Sri Lanka 120. China 169. Pakistan
6	Inclusive Development Index, 2018	World Economic Forum 22nd Jan. 2018	74	1. Norway 2. Iceland 3. Luxembourg	74. Mozambique 73. Lesotho 72. Malawi	62 (60 in 2017)	34. Bangladesh 40. Sri Lanka 47. Pakistan

7	Global Talent Competitiveness Index, 2018	INSEED 22nd Jan, 2018	119	1. Switzerland 2. Singapore 3. U.S.A.	119. Yemen 118. Madagascar 117. Mozambique	81 (92 in 2017)	43. China 82. Sri Lanka 109. Pakistan
8	Corruption Perception Index, 2018	Transparency International 21st January 2018	180	1. New Zealand 2. Denmark 3. Finland	180. Somalia 178. S. Sudan 178. Syria	81 (79 in 2017)	79. China 117. Pakistan 143. Bangladesh
9	Global Manufacturing Index, 2018	World Economic Forum 14th Jan. 2018	100	1. Japan 2. S. Korea 3. Germany	-- -- --	30	5. China 66. Sri Lanka 74. Pakistan
10	Climate Change Performance Index, 2019	German Watch and Climate Action Network, Europe 10th December 2018	56+EU	4. Sweden 5. Morocco 6. Lithuania	60. Saudi Arabia 59. USA 58. Iran	11 (14 in 2018)	33. China
11	Global Hunger Index (GHI) 2018	Concern World Wide and Wealth Hunger Hilfe 14th October 2018	119	Belarus, Bosnia, Herzegovina, Chile, Costa Rica, Croatia, Cuba, Astonia Kuwait, Latwia, Lithuania, Montenigro, Romania, Turkey, Eukrain, Uruguay	119. Central African Republic 118. Chad 117. Yemen	103 (100 in 2017)	25. China 72. Nepal 106. Pakistan
12	Global Competitiveness Index, 2018-19	World Economic Forum 19th October, 2018	140	1. U.S.A. 2. Singapore 3. Germany	140. Haiti 139. Yemen 138. Chad	58	109. Nepal 103. Bangladesh 107. Pakistan
13	Global Human Capital Report, 2017	World Economic Forum 13th September 2017	130	1. Norway 2. Finland 3. Switzerland	130. Yemen 129. Mauritania 128. Senegal	103	34. China 70. Sri Lanka 125. Pakistan

14	Modern Slavery Index 2017	Global Maple croft 10th August 2017	198	1. North Korea 2. Syria 3. South Sudan	133. Italy 129. Yunan 66. Romania	49 (Green Shoots of Progress)	
15	Global Cyber Security Index 2017	International Telecommunication Union 5th July, 2017	193	1. Singapore 2. U.S.A. 3. Malaysia	Ginny	23	32. China 53. Bangladesh 66. Pakistan
16	Global Retirement Index, 2018	Natixis Global 4th September 2018	43	1. Switzerland 2. Iceland 3. Norway	43. India 42. Brazil 41. Yunan	43	40. China
17	Sustainable Development Goal Index, 2018	Sustainable Development Solution Network, 7th July 2018	156	1. Sweden 2. Denmark 3. Finland	156. Central African Republic 155. Chad 154. Congo	112 (116 in 2017)	126. Pakistan 111. Bangladesh
18	Global Retail Development Index	A.T. Kearney 5th June 2017	30	1. India 2. China 3. Malaysia	30. Thailand 29. Brazil 28. Bolivia	1	12. Sri Lanka
19	Global Peace Index, 2018	Institute for Economics and Peace (EPI) 6th June 2018	163	1. Switzerland 2. New Zealand 3. Austria	163. Syria 162. Afghanistan 161. South Sudan	136	67. Sri Lanka 112. China 151. Pakistan
20	Global Innovation Index, 2018	INSEAD 10 July, 2018	126	1. Switzerland 2. Netherlands 3. Sweden	126. Yemen 125. Togo 124. Burcinafaso	57 (60 in 2017)	17. China 109. Pakistan 116. Bangladesh
21.	Fragile State Index, 2018	Foreign Policy and The Fund for Peace 24th April, 2018	178	1. South Sudan 2. Somalia 3. Yemen	178. Finland 177. Norway 176. Switzerland (Most Stable Countries)	72	9. Afghanistan 21. Pakistan 89. China

22	Renewable Energy Country Attractiveness Index, 2018	Ernest and Young 1st May 2018	40	1. China 2. U.S.A. 3. Germany	40. Kazakhstan 39. Kenya 38. Indonesia	4 (2 in 2017)	1. China 26. Pakistan
23	World Press Freedom Index 2018	Reporters Without Borders 25th April 2018	180	1. Norway 2. Sweden 3. Netherland	180. North Korea 179. Eritrea 178. Turkmenistan	138 (136 in 2017)	175. China 139. Pakistan
24.	FDI Confidence Index 2018	A.T. Kearney 3rd May 2018	25	1. U.S.A. 2. Canada 3. Germany	25. Brazil 24. Austria 23. Norway	11 (8 in 2017)	5. China
25	Human Development Index, 2018	United Nations Development Programme 14th September 2018	189	1. Norway 2. Switzerland 3. Australia	188. Central African Republic 189. Niger 187. South Sudan	130 (131 in 2017)	86. China 136. Bangladesh 150. Pakistan
26	Global Connectivity Index, 2018	Huawei (China) 31st may, 2018	80	1. U.S.A. 2. Singapore 3. Sweden	80. Ethiopia 79. Bangladesh 78. Pakistan	64 (63 in 2017)	27. China
27	Travel and Tourism Competitiveness Index, 2017	World Economic Forum 5th April 2017	136	1. Spain 2. France 3. Germany	136. Yemen 135. Chad 134. Burundi	40	15. China 78. Bhutan 124. Pakistan
28	Economic Freedom Index, 2018	The Heritage Foundation and Wall Street Journal 12th April, 2018	186	1. Hong Kong 2. Singapore 3. New Zealand	180. North Korea 179. Venezuela 178. Cuba	130 (143 in 2017)	131. Pakistan 128. Bangladesh 110. China

29	IMD Talent Rankings, 2017	International Institute of Management (IMD) 20th November 2017	63	1. Switzerland 2. Denmark 3. Belgium	63. Venezuela 62. Mongolia 61. Romania	51 (54 in 2016)	40. China 43. Russia
30	Global Terrorism Index, 2018	Institute for Economics and Peace December 2018	163	1. Iraq 2. Afghanistan 3. Nigeria		7 (8 in 2017)	5. Pakistan 25. Bangladesh 36. China
31	Global Gender Gap Report, 2018	World Economic Forum 18th December 2018	149	1. Iceland 2. Norway 3. Sweden	149. Yemen 148. Pakistan 147. Syria	108 (108 also in 2017)	48. Bangladesh 103. China 105. Nepal
32	Ease of doing Business Index, 2019	World Bank 31st October 2018	190	1. New Zealand 2. Singapore 3. Denmark	190. Somalia 189. Eritrea 188. Venezuela	77 (100 in 2018)	46. China 110. Nepal 136. Pakistan

Books for Preliminary Examination

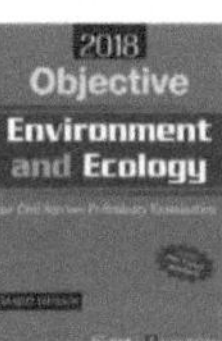

Books for Main Examination

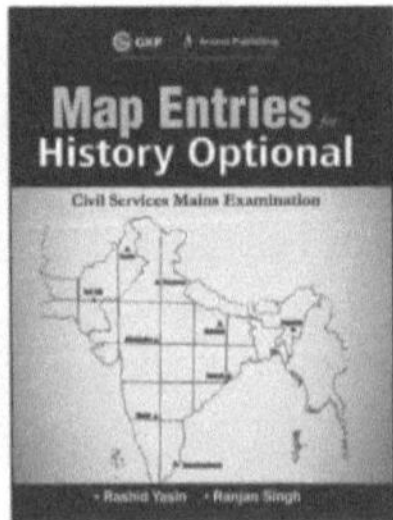

ACCESS			
ISBN	**TITLE**	**AUTHOR**	**PRICE**
UPSC - Civil Services Preliminary and Main Examinations			
General Books			
9789389161106	Current Affairs - A Ready Reckoner for (2019-20)	Rashid Yasin & Amit Jha	195.00
9789387766792	Current Affairs - A Ready Reckoner (2018)	Mohammad Rizwan	160.00
9789383454761	Cracking the Civil Services Exam: The Open Secret	Ashok Kumar	175.00
9789383454884	Civil Sewa Pariksha Apki Muthi Mein: Safalta Hetu Tips and Techniques	Ashok Kumar	175.00
Text Books (English)			
9789388182133	History of Modern India (2e)	Sujata Menon	395.00
9789386860415	General Science for Preliminary Examination, 2018	N K Bajaj	495.00
9789386860392	Economic and Social Development for Preliminary Examination, 2018	S Maitra	350.00
9789388030786	Indian Economy (4e)	S Maitra	725.00
9789383454204	The Constitution of India - Bare Act with Short Notes	A R Khan	175.00
9789383454693	Indian and World Geography (2e)	D R Khullar	465.00
9789389161649	Indian Heritage, Art and Culture (2e) - Multicolour	Madhukar Bhagat	435.00
9789387766488	Environment & Ecology - A Dynamic Approach	Neeraj Nachiketa	400.00
9789389161045	Environment & Ecology - A Dynamic Approach (Marathi)	Neeraj Nachiketa	450.00
9789386860422	Essentials of Polity & Governance in India	N D Arora	450.00
9789383454723	Physical, Human and Economic Geography	D R Khullar	240.00
9789383454730	World Geography for Main Examination	D R Khullar	650.00
9789387444249	Environment & Ecology (4e)	Majid Husain	510.00
9789388426381	Ethics, Integrity & Aptitude (4e) for Main Examination, 2019	G Subba Rao	599.00
9789388030502	Economic Development in India (2e)	Access	495.00
9789386601759	Social Problems, Women Empowerment, Population Issues and Diversity of India for Main Examination	Bitasta Das	325.00
9789386601919	Comprehensive World History for Main Examination	Sujata Menon	425.00
Text Books (Hindi)			
9789388426282	Bharatiya Virasat, Kala evam Sanskriti	Madhukar Bhagat	350.00

9789388426565	Neetishastra, Satyanishtha evam Abhivriti, 2019(Hindi)	G. Subba Rao	599.00
9789387444324	Paryavaran evam Paristhitiki (4e)	Majid Husain	510.00
9789388426640	Bharat ka Bhugol (2e) (Hindi)	Surender Singh	425.00
9789387766808	Environment & Ecology - A Dynamic Approach (Hindi)	Neeraj Nachiketa	450.00
9789388030823	Bharatiya Arthvyavastha (3e)	Dr. Kriti Rastogi	395.00
9789388182577	Bharatiya Kala, Sanskriti evam Virasat (2e)	Meenakshi Kant	395.00
Objective Series (English)			
9789388030687	Objective Economy	Access	245.00
9789388030694	Objective Indian History & National Movement	Access	225.00
9789388030700	Objective Science & Technology	Access	225.00
9789387444218	Objective Indian & World Geography	D R Khullar	250.00
9789386860408	Objective Environment & Ecology	Majid Husain	325.00
9789386860385	Objective Indian Polity & Governance	N D Arora	350.00
Objective Series (Hindi)			
9789388030878	Vastunishth Arthvyavastha	Access	225.00
9789388030885	Vastunishth Bhartiya Itihaas evam Rashtriya Andolan	Access	225.00
9789388030892	Vastunishth Vigyaan evam Takniki	Access	225.00
9789386860576	Vastunishth Bharat evam Vishwa ka Bhugol	D R Khullar	225.00
9789386860569	Vastunishth Paryavaran evam Paristhitiki	Majid Hussain	275.00
9789388182775	Vasthunishth Prashn Sangrah - Bharat ki Rajvyavastha evam Shasan	N D Arora	250.00
9789386860620	Vastunishth Bharat ka Itihas	Meenakshi Kant	295.00
Preliminary Examination Preparation Books (English)			
9789389310153	UPSC Preliminary Examination 2020 - General Studies Paper I: 23 Years' Topic-wise Solved Papers (1997-2019)	Access	395.00
9789389310160	UPSC Preliminary Examination 2020 – General Studies Paper II (CSAT) Manual	V Sasikumar	995.00
9789389310122	UPSC Preliminary Examination 2020: CSAT Mantra	Access	450.00
9789389310139	UPSC Preliminary Examination 2020 Reading Comprehension (CSAT Paper II)	Ashok Kumar Singh	395.00
9789389310146	Logical Reasoning, Analytical Ability & GMA (4e) for CSAT (Paper II), 2020	Access	395.00
9789388182386	General Studies Paper I Manual, 2019	Access	1495.00
9789386860453	General Studies Paper II (CSAT) Manual, 2018	Access	795.00
9789388426916	Booster Test Series: 10 Mock Tests + 12 Topic Tests (General Studies Paper-I) 2019	Access	595.00

Preliminary Examination Preparation Books (Hindi)			
9789389310177	General Studies Paper II (CSAT) Manual 2020	V Sasikumar	995.00
9789388182454	Samanya Adhayayan Paper I 2019	Access	1495.00
9788193975503	Booster Test Series: 10 Mock Tests + 12 Topic Tests (General Studies Paper-I) 2019	Access	495.00
Study Guides - Main Examination			
9789389121995	Internal Security in India - Issues & Perspectives	Vivek TV	225.00
9789389121704	Complete History through Questions & Answers 2019	Rashid Yasin	495.00
9789388426572	Essays for Civil and Judicial Services Examinations, 2019	AP Bhardwaj	250.00
9789388030656	Map Entries for History Optional 2019	Rashid Yasin	175.00
9789388426398	UPSC Main Examination 2019 - General Studies Paper II	D V K Rao	495.00
9789387444409	Mastering Effective Reading Skills 2019	G Subba Rao	345.00
9789388426404	Compulsory English for IAS Mains & Judicial Services Examinations, 2019	Hari Mohan Prasad	450.00
9789388426596	UPSC Main Examination 2019 - Modern World History	Uddipan Mukherjee	295.00
9789388426497	UPSC Main Examination 2019 - India Map Entries	Majid Husain	325.00
9789388426619	UPSC Main Examination 2019 - Nibandh 2019 (Hindi)	Sheelwant Singh	460.00
9789388426374	UPSC Main Examination 2019 - General Studies Paper III	D V K Rao	450.00
9789388426633	UPSC Main Examination 2019 - Geography of India (2e)	Surender Singh & Jitender Saroha	495.00
UPSC & State Civil Services Courseware			
9788194114406	UPSC Civil Services Courseware (2019-20) for Preliminary & Main Examinations (11 Books)	Access	2999.00
Solved Papers - Preliminary & Main Examination (English)			
9789389161977	UPSC Preliminary Examination 2020 - General Studies Paper I 23 Years' Solved Papers (1997-2019)	Access	395.00
9789389161960	UPSC Preliminary Examination 2020 - General Studies Paper II (CSAT) 25 Years' Solved Papers (1995-2019)	Access	275.00
9789388426558	UPSC Main Examination 2019 - General Studies Papers I-IV Solved Papers (2013-2018)	Access	275.00
9789388426145	UPSC Main Examination 2019 - IAS Mains Compulsory English Solved Papers (2001-18, 5e)	A P Bhardwaj	340.00

Solved Papers - Preliminary & Main Examination (Hindi)			
9789389161991	UPSC Preliminary Examination 2020 - General Studies Paper I 9 Years' Solved Papers (2011-2019, Hindi)	Access	175.00
9789389161984	UPSC Preliminary Examination 2020 - General Studies Paper II (CSAT) 9 Years' Solved Papers (2011-2019, Hindi)	Access	195.00
9789388426435	UPSC Main Examination 2019 - General Studies Paper I-IV Solved Papers (2013-2018)	Access	295.00
Practice Papers - Preliminary & Main Examination (English)			
9789389161946	UPSC Preliminary Examination 2020 - General Studies Paper I Topic-wise Objective Question Bank	Access	395.00
9789389161243	UPSC Preliminary Examination 2020 - General Studies Paper II (CSAT) 17 Practice Papers	Access	295.00
9789389161250	UPSC Preliminary Examination 2020 - General Studies Paper I 17 Practice Papers	Access	295.00
Practice Papers - Preliminary & Main Examination (Hindi)			
9789389161953	UPSC Preliminary Examination 2020 - General Studies Paper I Topic-wise Objective Question Bank (Hindi)	Access	395.00
9789389161267	UPSC Preliminary Examination 2020 - General Studies Paper II (CSAT) 17 Practice Papers (Hindi)	Access	295.00
9789389161274	UPSC Preliminary Examination 2020 - General Studies Paper I 17 Practice Papers (Hindi)	Access	295.00
State Services Examinations			
UPPCS			
9789388426299	UPPSC RO & ARO 2019 - Samanya Adhyayan Guide (Preliminary & Mains, 2e, Hindi)	Access	425.00
9789388426305	UPPSC RO & ARO 2019 - Samanya Adhyayan 32 Practice Sets (Preliminary & Mains, 2e, Hindi)	Access	275.00
9789388426275	UPPCS Main Examination 2019 Samanya Adhyayan 20 Mock Tests	Access	450.00
9789388030908	Booster Test Series: UPPCS General Studies Paper I & II 20 Mock Tests (Questions, Answers & Explanations)	Access	625.00
9789388030847	Booster Test Series: UPPCS General Studies Paper I 10 Mock Tests (Questions, Answers & Explanations)	Access	399.00

ISBN	Title	Author	Price
9789388030854	Booster Test Series: UPPCS General Studies Paper II 10 Mock Tests (Questions, Answers & Explanations)	Access	299.00
9789388426411	UPPCS 2019 - Previous Years' Topic-wise Solved Papers (Paper I (2003-18) & Paper II (2012-18))	Access	275.00
9789388426527	UPPCS Preliminary Examination 2019 Previous Years' Topic-wise Solved Papers Paper I (2003-18) & Paper II (2012-18)	Access	295.00
9788193975626	UPSSSC 2019 - Samanya Adhyayan - Combined Lower Subordinate Services Examination (Hindi)	Access	550.00
Punjab PCS			
9789387766891	Booster Test Series: Punjab PCS Examination (2018) 10 Mock Tests (Paper I & II)	Access	999.00
Himachal PCS			
9789389161656	Himachal (2019-20) A Complete Analysis for HAS (2e)	Nidhi Soni	540.00
WBCS			
9789388182140	WBCS General Studies - A Complete Manual	Access	950.00
Rajasthan PCS			
9789387444485	Rajasthan Naveen Samanya Gyan evam Samanya Vigyan	Sheelwant Singh & Rajeev Garg	550.00
MPPCS			
9789387444034	MP PSC Special - Madhya Pradesh General Knowledge	Rajeev Garg	225.00
9789388426060	Madhya Pradesh Sampoorna Samanya Adhyayan, 2019	Abhishek Khare	375.00
Static General Knowledge for All Exams			
9789387766518	Static General Knowledge	A P Bhardwaj	425.00

Printed by Libri Plureos GmbH in Hamburg, Germany